Parents as Friendship Coaches for Children with ADHD

This book introduces Parental Friendship Coaching (PFC), an intervention that parents can use to support peer relationships in their elementary school-aged children with ADHD.

In the PFC program, clinicians work with parents to coach their children with ADHD in friendship behaviors that help develop and maintain high-quality relationships. Featuring 10 research-based clinical sessions, the book provides detailed, step-by-step instructions for clinicians about intervention provision. Each session includes skills teaching devoted to supporting children's peer relationships, activities to practice the skills in session, problem-solving about difficulties carrying out the skills, and homework to try the skills at home. This book also includes handouts for parents and clinicians, tips for clinicians about addressing common parent difficulties, and suggestions for progress monitoring.

Intended for mental health professionals working with families of children with ADHD and peer problems, this book will aid clinicians in educating parents on how to support their children's friendship development.

Amori Yee Mikami, PhD, RPsych, is a professor of psychology at the University of British Columbia, Canada. Her program of research focuses on understanding and supporting children with ADHD and peer problems.

Sébastien Normand, PhD, CPsych, is an associate professor of psychology at the Université du Québec en Outaouais and a pediatric psychologist at Hôpital Montfort, Canada. His research focuses on children with ADHD.

"The authors have crafted what I consider to be the best program currently available for working with children with ADHD and their parents on improving the children's peer relationships that are impaired in the majority of such children. Why? Other social skills programs that predate this one were not designed expressly for the social difficulties evident in children with ADHD. This one was, given that it is based on all that research has taught us about what is going wrong in those peer relationships. The others were based on children with other conditions, usually social anxiety, whereas this one is directly focused on ADHD. The other programs are based on a faulty premise—that children with ADHD are ignorant of social skills and, because they don't know them, must be trained in them. This program gets it right—ADHD creates more of a problem with using the knowledge and skills a child has in everyday social relationships, and not regarding ignorance of knowledge. Furthermore, other programs train children in artificial circumstances, such as clinics, usually involving other children the child does not normally encounter in their daily life—so they don't generalize much if at all to natural social settings, if they work at all. For all these and other reasons, there is no better source than this one for working with families of children with ADHD. Every discipline interested in doing so will benefit greatly from making this program available."

Russell A. Barkley, PhD, *clinical professor of psychiatry, School of Medicine, Virginia Commonwealth University; editor, Attention-Deficit Hyperactivity Disorder: A Handbook for Diagnosis and Treatment (4ᵗʰ ed.).*

"This guide is a wonderful gift to clinicians, filling the enormous need for resources to improve the peer relationships of children with ADHD. Based on years of rigorous research, the *Parental Friendship Coaching* program uses a behavioral parent training approach to improve social interactions. This comprehensive, practical guide is an essential resource for mental health clinicians in school, primary care, and clinical settings, as well as graduate students preparing to be clinicians and researchers."

Thomas J. Power, PhD, ABPP, *distinguished endowed chair in the Department of Pediatrics; director, Center for Management of ADHD, Children's Hospital of Philadelphia, University of Pennsylvania; co-author, Homework Success for Children with ADHD: A Family-School Intervention Program.*

"Problems with acquiring and maintaining high-quality friendships are a major source of distress for children with ADHD. *Parental Friendship Coaching* is a unique and innovative program that addresses this. The manual for teaching parents how to support their children with peer relations is rich with strategies based on clinical experience and research. Clinicians who work with children with ADHD should have *Parental Friendship Coaching* in their intervention repertoire."

Judith Wiener, PhD, CPsych, *professor emerita, Department of Applied Psychology and Human Development, OISE/University of Toronto; co-author, Psychological Assessment of Culturally and Linguistically Diverse Children and Adolescents: A Practitioner's Guide.*

"Mikami and Normand present a very authoritative manual for a parent-mediated intervention to help children with ADHD experiencing difficulties in relationships with friends. At least half of the population of children with ADHD need help in this area and could benefit from this timely book. The program described is for parents working under the guidance of a helping professional, whether in a parent-group format or as a family. Although the material distributed to parents is specific enough to stand on its own, the clinician's judgment provides for personalization and flexibility. The manual contains the details needed for the program to be implemented with integrity, maintaining focus on the behaviors needed to form and make friends. The language used is specific and accessible but not excessively simplistic. The emphasis on empirical evidence is a distinct strength of the program. Materials are provided to evaluate each implementation in a systematic way. The time needed for the evaluation is flexible and by no means excessive. The authors are candid about the empirical foundation of the program: It has been shown to improve the behaviors associated with positive friendship, which is impressive. The program's effect on the subjective aspects of friendship quality has yet to be proven. Thus, the program can be seen as bringing the child with ADHD into a position where the natural processes of attraction between friends may take over and bring rewarding, close relationships."

Barry H. Schneider, PhD, *professor emeritus, School of Psychology, University of Ottawa; senior lecturer, Department of Psychology and Neuroscience, Boston College; author, Childhood Friendships and Peer Relations: Friends and Enemies.*

Parents as Friendship Coaches for Children with ADHD

A Clinical Guide

Amori Yee Mikami
and
Sébastien Normand

Routledge
Taylor & Francis Group

NEW YORK AND LONDON

First published 2022
by Routledge
605 Third Avenue, New York, NY 10158

and by Routledge
2 Park Square, Milton Park, Abingdon, Oxon, OX14 4RN

Routledge is an imprint of the Taylor & Francis Group, an informa business

© 2022 Amori Yee Mikami and Sébastien Normand

Library of Congress Cataloging-in-Publication Data
A catalog record has been requested for this book

ISBN: 978-1-032-11831-4 (hbk)
ISBN: 978-1-032-11828-4 (pbk)
ISBN: 978-1-003-22171-5 (ebk)

DOI: 10.4324/9781003221715

Typeset in Times New Roman
by Newgen Publishing UK

Access the Support Material: Routledge.com/9781032118284

To all children who are perceived as different by their peers, for whatever reason, and to the parents who create inclusive spaces for these kids with acceptance, perseverance, and kindness.

A.Y.M.

To my step-daughter Élisabeth Brosda (1995–2016) who reminds me every day about the urgency of love.

S.N.

Contents

Acknowledgments

This clinical guide is based on research supported by the National Institute of Mental Health (1R03MH 079019), the Canadian Institutes of Health Research (CIHR MOP-125897), and the Michael Smith Foundation for Health Research Scholar Award; the opinions expressed are those of the authors and do not represent views of the funding sources. We express our appreciation to the many graduate and undergraduate research assistants, clinicians, collaborators, and schools who contributed to conducting this research. Finally, we are grateful to the families who participated in these studies and whose feedback helped us improve the Parental Friendship Coaching program. Without their inspiration, and their efforts, this work could not have been done.

PARENTAL
FRIENDSHIP
COACHING

Introduction for Clinicians

Welcome

Welcome to the Parental Friendship Coaching (PFC) program! The goal of this program is to support children with attention-deficit/hyperactivity disorder (ADHD) who have social problems, such as poor social skills and peer relationships, through working with their parents. PFC focuses on teaching parents how to coach their children in developing better friendships. The intervention consists of 10 sessions delivered to parents, and no direct intervention by the clinician with the child.

Who Is the Audience for This Clinical Guide?

This clinical guide is intended for mental health professionals working with families of children with ADHD and peer problems. This includes (but is not limited to) clinical psychologists, counseling psychologists, school psychologists, school counselors, licensed clinical social workers, and marriage and family therapists. This guide could also be used by students in these same fields, with supervision to implement therapy in training settings. It is highly recommended that clinicians have a background in behavioral parent training interventions, generally and specific to ADHD, to be able to implement PFC. Readers interested in learning about behavioral parent training interventions can find more information in the following references:

Barkley, R. A. (2013). *Defiant children: A clinician's manual for assessment and parent training.* Guilford Press.
* *This reference is also available in Spanish, Italian, Dutch, and Romanian.*

Chorpita, B. F., & Weisz, J. R. (2009). *MATCH-ADTC: Modular approach to therapy for children with anxiety, depression, trauma, or conduct problems.* PracticeWise, LLC.
This reference is also available in Spanish, French, and German.

DOI: 10.4324/9781003221715-1

Chronis-Tuscano, A., O'Brien, K., & Danko, C. M. (2021). *Supporting caregivers of children with ADHD: An integrated parenting program.* Oxford University Press.

Kazdin, A. E. (2005). *Parent management training: Treatment for oppositional, aggressive, and antisocial behavior in children and adolescents.* Oxford University Press.

Laver-Bradbury, C., Thompson, M., Weeks, A., Daley, D., & Sonuga-Barke, E. J. S. (2010). *Step by step help for children with ADHD: A self-help manual for parents.* Jessica Kingsley Publishers.

McMahon, R. J., & Forehand, R. L. (2003). *Helping the noncompliant child: Family-based treatment for oppositional behavior* (2nd ed.). Guilford Press.

Webster-Stratton, C. (2019). *The Incredible Years®: Trouble shooting guide for parents of children aged 3–8 years* (3rd ed.). Incredible Years.

*This reference is also available in Spanish.

For Which Families Do We Recommend PFC?

PFC is for families of elementary school-age children with ADHD who show social problems with peers, and where the parents are seeking skills to support their children in this area. The types of social problems that are most responsive to PFC are child behaviors with friends on playdates, such as difficulty with: attending to the friend's needs, sharing, following game rules, being a good winner or a good loser, noticing when the friend is bored or upset, negotiating, problem-solving, and controlling temper outbursts. These are common problems in children with ADHD, and especially for those children with co-occurring externalizing problems, such as aggressive and argumentative behavior.

PFC is ideally suited for parents who witness their child doing these types of behaviors with peers, and want to do something about them, but feel at a loss about what to do. Perhaps the parent has tried to talk to the child about the behaviors, but this only leads to arguments, or, despite having talked about it, the child forgets about what the parent says in the heat of the moment with the friend. PFC is specifically designed to address these sorts of situations. Because the parent is asked to make a substantial investment in coaching the child, setting up playdates, and practicing skills with the child, PFC is best suited for parents who are willing and able to take on these tasks.

Parents who benefit most from PFC often have children who are not brand new to diagnosis of ADHD. They have had the opportunity to receive answers to the questions parents typically have when their children are first diagnosed. Most likely they have tried other treatments for ADHD, but those treatments have not fully addressed their child's social problems, even if the treatments may have helped with symptom reduction or other ADHD-related impairments. Because PFC applies behavioral treatment principles to social problems, it is also helpful when parents have been exposed to behavioral parent training previously. These parents are ready to intensively address social problems in their children using behavioral methods.

Why Treat Social Problems?

Social problems are common and affect 50–80% of children with ADHD. Furthermore, social problems hurt. Although children may not always admit it, many know when they are disliked by peers or friendless. Far from motivating children with ADHD to improve their behavior, poor peer relationships instead lead to loneliness, anxiety, conduct problems, and even academic failure as school becomes an unpleasant place. The negative consequences of longstanding social problems often compound over time as a child becomes a teenager, and can last into adulthood. Third, social problems do not necessarily respond to more general interventions to manage ADHD symptoms, such as medication or behavior management. In many cases, although the ADHD symptoms are improved, social problems remain and thus require a tailored approach.

Children with ADHD can have many different types of social problems, but the PFC program focuses on improving friendship. Friendship is a mutual relationship between two children. Unfortunately, many children with ADHD show poor behaviors with friends, as described above, such as being a poor sport, bossiness, emotional outbursts, demanding that they get their way, ignoring the friend, or not noticing the friend's needs. Because of these behaviors, many children with ADHD have few friends, friendships which dissolve quickly, or poor emotional bonds with their friends. Children with ADHD are also more likely to be friends with peers who also have attention, learning, behavior, and/or social problems than typical children. Importantly, such problem behaviors in their friends often lead to poorer friendships.

Working to improve friendships can provide children with many benefits. A good friendship provides a motivating context for children to learn and practice important social skills that can generalize to other social situations. Friends also help children feel less lonely and more connected to school and can provide social support to buffer other difficult situations or transitions that the child may be experiencing. Finally, having supportive friends can reduce risk for other types of social problems, such as bulling/ victimization, and peer rejection. Friendships are also known to protect children from other environmental and biological risk factors, including natural disasters, chronic illness, and genetic risk for depressive symptoms. Growing research is documenting these positive benefits of having a good friend, particularly for children with ADHD.

Why Work with Parents?

Social problems in children with ADHD have also not been responsive, in general, to clinic-based social skills training. PFC has the philosophy that parents are in the best position to coach their children with ADHD regarding friendships because, unlike clinicians, they are in the child's life for the long term, and they see the child in real-world social situations with peers (mainly during playdates). The overarching goal of PFC is to teach parents to coach their children in friendship skills and to provide a context for children to practice those skills on playdates. In the longer term, the aim is for children to develop better friendships, which can result in social competence with other peers besides just that friend, and better adjustment in other areas as well (such as less loneliness, anxiety, or depression).

Social problems do not exist in a vacuum where only the child with ADHD contributes to them. Rather, the values and norms of the community, school, neighborhood, family, and the other peers all matter in affecting why a child with ADHD may have friends versus be friendless. Potentially, working with parents could target these broader contextual factors. We also hope that working with parents may be more empowering to parents by asking them to take an active role in their child's social development and be less stigmatizing to the children with ADHD than other child-directed interventions they receive.

There are three topic areas in PFC, which are in the Outline of Sessions and in the PFC Pyramid graphic in the Session 1 handouts (see Appendix B).

1   Increase children's receptiveness to parental guidance. The aim is to lay a foundation that will help children to receive their parents' guidance, through building a positive parent–child relationship and helping parents learn to deliver their feedback in strategic ways. Most parents have had the experience where they try to give their child guidance, but their child is defensive and puts up a wall. The first few sessions are heavily devoted to this topic, because everything else rests on the child being receptive to parental guidance.
2   Teach children social skills. Parents learn how to teach their children specific social skills that are key to friendship making and commonly impaired among children with ADHD. These are the same types of skills that clinicians often teach children with ADHD. But a common problem is that after children leave the clinician's office, they forget to implement the skills in real-life peer situations. The reason we have the parent do the skill teaching is because the parent continues to be around to reinforce and remind the child to implement the skills, until it eventually becomes more natural and automatic for the child. This topic is introduced midway through the 10 sessions.
3   Arrange social opportunities for children. Parents arrange social situations where their children will be able (and likely) to carry out the social skills that the parent has been teaching them. This involves the parent arranging structured, fun playdates for the child with peers who are inclined to get along with the child, where the parent can monitor to intervene in case things are starting to go badly. This step is important to give the child a chance to practice these new social skills in a structured and positive setting. This topic is introduced midway through the 10 sessions and emphasized more as the sessions progress.

We encourage clinicians to share the philosophy of PFC with parents before embarking on the specific program strategies, and this is written into Session 1. Because it can be overwhelming for parents to hear this all at once in the first session, as clinicians introduce new topics, it can help to remind parents of how the topic fits within the PFC Pyramid.

An outline of session topics is below.

Session	Title	Topics
1	**Understanding Your Child's Social Behaviors**	• Increase parent awareness of child's friendships • Introduce model that parents can affect friendships (Antecedents, Behavior, Consequences [ABC] model) • Build parent–child relationship so children accept parent feedback, Part 1 (Special Time)
2	**Giving Effective Feedback to Your Child about Social Behaviors**	• Build parent–child relationship so children accept parent feedback, Part 2 (active listening) • Help parent give guidance about social behaviors, Part 1 (labeled praise)
3	**Helping Your Child to Choose the Right Friends**	• Help parent give guidance about social behaviors, Part 2 (effective corrective feedback) • Parent identifies appropriate potential friends for child
4	**Preparing for a Playdate as a Host, Part 1**	• Help parent handle child defiance to parent's guidance about social conduct • Parent prepares child for a playdate as a host, Part 1 (preventing boredom)
5	**Teaching Your Child Social Skills, Part 1**	• Parent teaches child good friendship skills, Part 1 (game-playing skills, good sport) • Parent prepares child for a playdate as a host, Part 2 (preventing conflict)
6	**Preparing for a Playdate as a Host, Part 2**	• Parent teaches child good friendship skills, Part 2 (conversational skills) • Help parent intervene in playdate when boredom and conflict occur
7	**Teaching Your Child Social Skills, Part 2**	• Parent teaches child good friendship skills, Part 3 (emotion regulation) • Parent learns to effectively debrief with child after the playdate

Session	Title	Topics
8	**Preparing for a Playdate as a Guest**	• Parent prepares child for playdates as a guest • Parent learns to check in with the other family after a playdate as guest
9	**Meeting New Peers**	• Parent assists child in meeting new potential friends • Parent networks with other parents to build social contacts for the child
10	**Getting Ready for the Future**	• Help parent decide whether to have another playdate with the same friend • Discuss how to continue working on building good friendships

How to Use This Clinical Guide?

This clinical guide consists of 10 sessions, with the flexibility for being delivered in either group or individual format. A group format has the benefit of potentially allowing parents to receive and provide social support, to feel hopeful and empowered, and to learn from other parents who are facing similar issues in their children. We recommend that group sessions are 90 minutes in length. In our work, groups consisting of six to seven families (where one or two caregivers attend from each family) has been an ideal size. An individual format has the benefit of allowing clinicians to tailor the topics and strategies to fit a given family's unique needs. We have found that the content can be completed in individual sessions of 50–60 minutes.

The timing of sessions is also flexible. We recommend one week or more between sessions to allow parents time to internalize the skills and carry out the homework. However, parents' individual needs will differ, and clinicians are invited to adjust the program pace accordingly.

Each section begins with a summary for the clinician about the overarching goal of that section. We encourage clinicians to share this goal with parents, and it can also help clinicians make decisions about whether a discussion is tangential to the goal of the section. Each section also includes a summary of things for which clinicians should be watchful, based on our experience with PFC. There are labeled sections on homework review (Session 2 onward), specific topics, and ending business.

Each topic is structured so that the clinician first states the problem that they are trying to address (e.g., your child gets really upset about small things, and can go from 0 to 60 in an instant), and then checks in with parents about whether, and how, this problem manifests in their child. Next, the clinician presents information about why the problem gets in the way of social relationships (e.g., this emotional roller coaster can be upsetting to your child, it can turn off peers, it can make everyone feel like they are walking on eggshells). Finally, the clinician explains how the skill being taught is meant to address the problem, and where this skill falls within the PFC Pyramid (i.e., the three topic areas in PFC). At the end of each topic, there is a section for special considerations if PFC is being administered in group format.

Each topic has a number of associated role-plays and/or video recording reviews to encourage parent engagement with the material and to help parents actively practice the skills. It is useful for the clinician to be aware that these activities are sometimes anxiety-provoking for parents, and potentially, to acknowledge the discomfort. The clinician might explain the rationale to parents that people learn more by doing than by passively listening, work to make a safe environment where mistakes are ok, and praise parents for being brave to try role-plays. At first, it can be helpful for the parent to play the "child" in the role-play instead of playing the parent (who must demonstrate the skills), and the clinician can play the "parent." If a group format is chosen, all the parents can collaborate together (e.g., multi-headed parent) to tag team the role of the parent so that no single parent is on the spot. When the clinician or other parents offer feedback after role-plays and/or video recording reviews, it is important to focus on parents' strengths, and especially in the first half of the program to build parents' confidence and empowerment. Eventually, and typically in the second half of the program, the clinician may invite the parent to share what they would do differently next time or ask any question to the group. Clinicians should do whatever they can so that role-play and video recording reviews are set up to encourage social support.

There is a lot of didactic material to get through in PFC. However, as much as time permits, the clinician is encouraged to help parents to come to their own conclusions, instead of telling the parent the "right" answers. We have found that this helps to empower parents and to keep them engaged with the material, which prepares them better to carry out the skills at home. If a group format is used, group members can share suggestions with one another, and brainstorm through difficult challenges, regarding how to carry out the skills.

Each PFC session is accompanied by handouts (which are located in Appendix B of this clinical guide and can be photocopied, or can be downloaded from the Routledge website). We have found it helpful for the clinician to print the handouts for the parent and to give the parent a binder where they can easily store the handouts from each session. It may be best for clinicians to give the handouts one session at a time, to make the program less overwhelming and more individualized (in case some handouts need to be tailored), and to keep parents focused on the content of the week. The parent can be asked to bring the binder back each time.

Tailoring Material to Parents' Individual Needs

Like most manualized interventions, there is a balance between sticking to the clinical guide content (which is what has been empirically tested) relative to tailoring content to individual needs (which can be more personalized, and increase parent buy-in and engagement with the program). We acknowledge that many clinicians have a lot of experience with navigating this balance.

Based on our experience, we want to call attention to several ways where it can be possible to tailor PFC to parents' individual concerns. We recognize that all these things are easier if PFC is being delivered in an individual format.

- In role-plays, have parents practice the skills that are most relevant to their children. For example, in the role-play about being a good host, have the parent practice the rule of "the guest is always right" if that is a problem for their child and ignore the rule of "be loyal to your guest" if that is not a problem for their child.
- In video recording reviews, tailor the clip selected and the feedback given based on the family's individual needs and treatment goals.
- Notice where it says "skip if not an issue" in the clinical guide. Go over these points when they are relevant to parents but skip or skim them if they are not relevant.

When teaching each topic, we recommend explicitly encouraging parents to reflect on their personal situation as much as possible.

- Ask parents how this information applies (or doesn't apply) to their child. Do they see their child as having these issues? What are any consequences of this issue for their child's peer relationships?
- Have parents identify the skill/activity from the section or handout that they would like to try working on with their child.
- Ask parents what barriers they anticipate when trying to implement the skill/activity with their child; these barriers may be different for different families.
- Help parents identify what supports they need to overcome any barriers to implementation of the skill/activity.

Encouraging Homework Completion

Doing "home practices" (or homework) is central to the theory of change in PFC. Parents need to try the skills at home with their children to see improvement. To encourage homework completion, we suggest a few things.

Check in with parents before they leave the session regarding what they are going to do for homework, when they are going to do it, and if they have questions or concerns about the assignment and its implementation. The Homework List handout in each session should help facilitate this process.

When reviewing the previous week's homework, start by asking parents to volunteer success stories about the homework, which may set a good tone. If a parent regularly seems to not be doing the homework, consider having a collaborative chat with that parent to ask why. The clinician might ask, "how can I make homework assignments more relevant for your family?" or "how can I make homework assignments more realistic to complete?"

Especially when setting up playdates, parents may legitimately be trying to arrange a playdate, but the other family has not responded or the playdate they have arranged will not happen for several weeks. This situation is different from homework nonadherence. It is natural for parents to have variability in when they have their first playdate. We had the goal for all parents to have at least one good playdate before the end of the 10 sessions; some parents may have more.

Consider that some parents of children with ADHD have mental health concerns such as ADHD or depression, so they may have trouble with the organizational skills and motivation needed to carry out homework. They may also have negative associations with the word "homework" because of their own histories of school difficulties. It is important to be sensitive to this while also finding ways to support these parents in homework completion.

Encouraging Engagement and Connection

Based on our experience with PFC, we found that providing childcare during sessions helped reduce a practical barrier for attendance. Holding the sessions in a community center in the neighborhood, as opposed to in a hospital, university, or clinic, also made them more accessible to some families. Finally, when PFC was conducted in group format, we provided light snacks for the parents and the kids. We think this may have helped group cohesion and connection between parents and clinicians. We understand that these aspects may or may not be practical for every clinician, or fit every family's needs.

Summary

We developed the PFC program because we have seen many children with ADHD struggling with social problems, and we aspired to find a way to support them that might be more efficacious, more empowering, and also less stigmatizing, than other available approaches. We hope that clinicians and families find PFC to be useful, practical, and relevant to their needs. Please send any feedback about how to further improve PFC to us at mikami@psych.ubc.ca (Amori Mikami) and sebastien.normand@uqo.ca (Sébastien Normand).

Background and Research

Background

Parental Friendship Coaching (PFC) is based upon the well-established behavioral parent training model for families of children with attention-deficit/hyperactivity disorder (ADHD). Behavioral parent training has existed for decades and has been pioneered by eminent ADHD researchers. There is a wealth of research supporting its utility in changing parenting practices to shape desirable behaviors, and reduce undesirable behaviors, in children with ADHD. Behavioral parent training can help to improve all sorts of child behaviors from engaging in morning routine more efficiently to completing homework without whining and complaining.

In PFC, many of the same strategies that are in behavioral parent training are used, but they specifically target improving children's social behaviors with their friends on playdates. Therefore, PFC is a specialized approach to treat children's peer problems, as opposed to other types of problems experienced by children with ADHD. The idea is that behavioral parent training is a useful and empirically supported intervention following strong principles, and to change social problems, these principles need to be tailored more closely to the friendship context.

PFC also contains components that are not included in typical behavioral parent training. These involve helping parents to network with other parents, to identify peers who would be potential friends for their child, to arrange playdates for their child, and to supervise the playdate in such a way that encourages friendships. Some of these ideas were inspired by the Program for the Education and Enrichment of Relational Skills (PEERS®) and its earlier iterations. For more information, see:

Frankel, F. D., & Myatt, R. J. (2003). *Children's friendship training.* Routledge.
Laugeson, E. A., & Frankel, F. (2010). *Social skills for teenagers with developmental and autism spectrum disorders: The PEERS treatment manual.* Routledge.

Research Trials of PFC

We have conducted research trials of PFC in the United States (2006–2009) and in Canada (2013–2018). The first was a pilot test of PFC which

DOI: 10.4324/9781003221715-2

took place in Virginia, United States. In this trial, 62 families of children with ADHD (ages 6–10) were randomized to either receive PFC (in group format, with once weekly sessions of 90 minutes) or to be in a no-treatment control condition. At post-treatment, the families were re-assessed. Among those who had received PFC, parents and teachers reported the children to have better friendship behaviors, compared to those in the control condition. Observed changes in less negative and more positive parenting were found as a result of PFC, and these changes in parenting were suggested to mediate some of the beneficial outcomes for the children. Importantly, parents thought that PFC was useful for their child's needs and were satisfied with the program. All in all, there were some positive results from this initial trial, in that changes were found not only on parent report but also on teacher report and observations; teachers and observers were kept unaware of who was given PFC versus who was in the control group. These findings led the two most recent evidence base updates published by the Society of Clinical Child and Adolescent Psychology to consider PFC as a "well-established" approach for treating social problems in children with ADHD (Evans et al., 2014, 2018).

The second trial aimed to test PFC under more rigorous conditions. We enrolled 172 families of children with ADHD (ages 6–11) in either Vancouver or Ottawa/Gatineau (representing western and eastern Canada). The families were randomized to either PFC or to a comparison intervention, known as Coping with ADHD through Relationships and Education (CARE). In CARE, parents were provided psychoeducation from clinicians, and parents were encouraged to support one another with strategies and tips. Both PFC and CARE were delivered in group format, for equivalent amounts of time (90-minute, weekly sessions). The families were re-assessed at post-treatment and at a follow-up eight months after. We evaluated PFC using more stringent measures, such as observations of child behaviors and friendship quality, that were not in the initial pilot of PFC. Relative to those in the CARE condition, children in the PFC condition showed better behaviors with their friends (observed and parent-reported, but not teacher-reported). On average, the children in PFC did not show any difference from those in CARE in friendship quality. However, it appeared that PFC helped friendship quality in certain at-risk subgroups of children with ADHD: those with co-occurring externalizing disorders and those whose families had received psychosocial treatment before. In addition, PFC resulted in more positive parenting, on observations, and children showing less withdrawn/depressed behaviors as reported by parents and teachers. Some of these outcomes maintained, or were present for the first time, at the eight-month follow-up. Parents receiving PFC were highly satisfied with the program and reported it to be a useful approach for their family.

In summary, based on the research, PFC appears to be useful for improving friendship behaviors which are often impaired in children with ADHD. These are behaviors such as sharing, taking turns, negotiating when the child and peer want to do different things, being a good sport, following game rules, paying attention to the peer's feelings, reading social cues that the peer is bored or upset, and controlling temper tantrums, during activities with friends such as playdates. PFC also seems to improve parent–child relationships and parents' positivity with their children, especially when parents are trying to give their child guidance about social skills. This is another area in which families of children with ADHD often need support.

However, the evidence right now is mixed about whether PFC directly results in better friendship quality (positive emotional bonds between a child and friend). On average, our research would suggest this is not the case. However, PFC may be helpful for improving friendship quality among children with ADHD and externalizing comorbidities, and/or children whose families have received psychosocial treatment before. We speculate this may be because these children require a specialized treatment for social problems such as PFC, as their social problems are more severe or they have not responded to other treatment. Parents who have experienced psychosocial treatment previously, especially if it is behavioral parent training, may also be more prepared to implement the skills and homework in PFC. On the other hand, if a family is new to treatment and/or new to the diagnosis of ADHD, even if their child also has social problems, we recommend beginning with a less specialized program such as one that provides psychoeducation about ADHD and behavioral parent training. If social problems persist after a general treatment is tried, then we recommend progressing to PFC.

Ongoing research is also currently looking at parent mental health and friend behavioral characteristics that could also be important to consider when working with families in PFC. Interested readers will find more about these studies when available on the authors' lab websites: (https://peerlab.psych.ubc.ca and https://irpcmh.uqo.ca). These studies will inform future versions of the current clinical guide. Future work will also assess whether and how cultural factors might influence PFC outcomes. There may be differences in whether and how playdates occur across cultures (as well as urban versus suburban versus rural environments). Additional research is needed to better tailor PFC for diverse populations and settings, including its implementation in telehealth. For more information, see:

Evans, S. W., Owens, J. S., & Bunford, N. (2014). Evidence-based psychosocial treatments for children and adolescents with attention-deficit/hyperactivity disorder. *Journal of Clinical Child and Adolescent Psychology, 43*(4), 527–551. https://doi.org/10.1080/15374416.2013.850700

Evans, S. W., Owens, J. S., Wymbs, B. T., & Ray, A. R. (2018). Evidence-based psychosocial treatments for children and adolescents with attention deficit/hyperactivity disorder. *Journal of Clinical Child and Adolescent Psychology, 47*(2), 157–198. https://doi.org/10.1080/15374416.2017.1390757

Mikami, A. Y., Jack, A., Emeh, C. C., & Stephens, H. F. (2010). Parental influences on children with attention-deficit/hyperactivity disorder: I. Parental behaviors associated with children's peer relationships. *Journal of Abnormal Child Psychology, 38*(6), 721–736. https://doi.org/10.1007/s10802-010-9393-2

Mikami, A. Y., Lerner, M. D., Griggs, M. S., McGrath, A., & Calhoun, C. D. (2010). Parental influences on children with attention-deficit/hyperactivity disorder: II. A pilot intervention training parents as friendship coaches for their children. *Journal of Abnormal Child Psychology, 38*(6), 737–749. https://doi.org/ 10.1007/s10802-010-9403-4

Mikami, A. Y., Normand, S., Hudec, K. L., Guiet, J., Na, J. J., Smit, S., Khalis, A., & Maisonneuve, M.-F. (2020). Treatment of friendship problems in children with attention-deficit/hyperactivity disorder: Initial results from a randomized clinical trial. *Journal of Consulting and Clinical Psychology, 88*(10), 871–885. https://doi.org/10.1037/ccp0000607

Smit, S., Mikami, A. Y., & Normand, S. (2022). Effects of the Parental Friendship Coaching intervention on parental emotion socialization of children with ADHD. *Research on Child and Adolescent Psychopathology, 50*(1), 101–115. https://doi.org/10.1007/s10802-021-00818-9

Clinical Provision of PFC

In addition to the evaluations in research trials, PFC has been piloted in several university and hospital clinics in the United States and Canada, with the goal of service provision. While all of the research trials have delivered PFC in group format (containing around six to seven families per group), the majority of the clinical pilots have used an individual format as opposed to a group format, and some have provided PFC in a half-day workshop. Although we have no efficacy data from these clinical pilot tests, these experiences suggest that it is feasible to adapt the format of PFC to individual sessions. Clinicians using an individual format provided PFC in sessions that were 50 minutes to 1 hour in length. Although clinicians generally completed the program in 10 sessions, they were able to increase or reduce the number of sessions, as needed by the family. The workshops were each 4 hours in length (including breaks) and provided key PFC skills and activities in abbreviated format. Satisfaction with the workshop was high, with all parents rating PFC as either "useful" or "very useful" for addressing their children's social problems.

Assessing Social Problems in Children

We offer recommendations for tools that clinicians can use to assess social problems in children with ADHD. When used to screen potential families, these questionnaires allow clinicians to know which children have the sorts of problems that are addressed by PFC. When administered at the beginning of treatment, they can help the clinician to better understand each family's unique issues and to personalize treatment. These same questionnaires can also be administered midway through or at the end of treatment, in order to monitor progress.

The following are four brief, and free, questionnaires for this purpose:

- Quality of Play Questionnaire, which has seven items focusing on negative friendship behaviors (i.e., aggressive/argumentative behavior) during playdates and is the most relevant to the treatment targets of PFC: available at https://link.springer.com/article/10.1007%2Fs10826-010-9437-9 (download the article and see the Appendix on pages 628–629 to get a copy of the measure).
- Friendship Quality Questionnaire, which has 40 items focusing on positive and negative features of the child's closest friendship: available at www.researchgate.net/publication/232540370 (download the article; see Table 1 to get items). The scale ranges from not at all true (0) to a little true (1) to somewhat true (2) to pretty true (3) to really true (4). This measure is also available at https://doi.org/10.1037/0012-1649.29.4.611
- Strengths and Questionnaire Difficulties Peer Problems subscale, containing five items about general peer problems (loneliness, friendship, victimization, rejection, doesn't get along with peers): available at www.sdqinfo.org (click on Questionnaires view and download, select language, select questionnaire version as per child age, and click on Scoring the SDQ tab for more information). This measure is available in several languages.
- Impairment Rating Scale peer items, which contains one item about friendship presence and one about general peer relationships. This measure has parent and teacher versions and is available at https://ccf.fiu.edu/research/_assets/impairment_rating_scales.pdf. This measure is available in several languages.

Other potentially useful questionnaires, which are copyrighted and available for purchase, are as follows:

- Conners 3 (short or long form) peer relations subscale, which contains between five and seven items that indicate children having difficulty with friendships, poor social skills, limited social connections, and poor peer acceptance. This measure has parent and teacher versions and is available at https://storefront.mhs.com/collections/conners-3. This measure is available in several languages.
- Child Behavior Checklist/Teacher Report Form 6–18 social problems subscale, containing 11 items about general social problems such as loneliness, victimization, rejection, and acting socially immature. This measure has parent and teacher versions and is available at https://store.aseba.org/School-Age-6-18-Materials/departments/11/. This measure is available in several languages.
- Social Skills Improvement System, which has 46 items (parent version) and 30 items (teacher version) about skilled social behaviors (e.g., cooperation, assertion, responsibility, empathy, self-control). This measure has parent and teacher versions and is available at

www.pearsonassessments.com/store/usassessments/en/Store/
Professional-Assessments/Behavior/Social-Skills-Improvement-
System-SSIS-Rating-Scales/p/100000322.html

If at all possible, we also recommend gathering some video recordings. At the beginning of treatment, we recommend asking the parent to take video of (a) them and their child talking about how to make and keep friends, and/or (b) the child interacting with a friend. Depending on the family's situation, it may be easier for the clinician to record the parent–child discussion at the clinician's office. The most feasible way to get video of the child interacting with a friend, however, is probably for the parent to record it during a playdate or other social interaction that their child is having.

If the parent is willing to create these recordings, this will help the clinician to understand the unique and real-life social issues and needs of the child and to assess the child's responses to parental coaching. Crucially, there are optional activities in the PFC clinical guide where the clinician and the parent review these videos together to illustrate skills being taught, and parents in the past have found this exercise extremely useful.

As treatment progresses, the clinician can ask the parent to take new videos of these same situations. The clinician can review these videos with the parent in session and also use them to monitor progress in terms of the child's display of good friendship behaviors and the parent's ability to coach the child. A limitation of this approach is that there is no easily-implemented objective coding system for these videos. We advise that the clinician might look for the following:

- A positive bond (warmth, shared laughter) between the parent and child or child and friend
- Negativity (criticism, harshness, disconnection, conflict) between the parent and child or child and friend
- The parent offering specific suggestions to the child about how to be a good friend, which the child can implement
- The helpful/prosocial versus argumentative behaviors between the child and friend
- Instances where the parent is demonstrating the PFC skills
- Places where the PFC skills might be useful

Although these videos are being used to support the family's treatment and are not for research purposes, it is still important to think about the confidentiality of the data. One consideration is whether those in the video know that the video is being recorded and for what purpose. Although it is not required by a research ethics board, we encourage the clinician to talk about this issue with parents and ask if the parent feels comfortable asking for consent to use the videos in this way from anyone in the recording (and the parents of other children in the recording). Recording a group in a public setting (e.g., the child's interactions with peers during soccer practice outside on a field) may feel different from recording a one-on-one playdate between the child and a friend, if the parent does not want to share the purpose of the video with those being recorded. A second consideration is where the video will be stored. If the parent keeps the video and brings it in to show the clinician in session, this will avoid the risk of someone else accidentally seeing the video on the clinician's phone or computer. However, the clinician will not be able to preview the video in advance to choose ideal clips for the exercises in this clinical guide. If the clinician keeps the video, then it is important for the clinician to store it in a secure manner.

Assessing Intervention Fidelity

To support clinicians with the implementation of the PFC content, an Intervention Fidelity Checklist for each session is included in Appendix A. The clinician can use the checklists during sessions to self-monitor the content that they are delivering in real time. Alternatively, the clinician could complete the checklists after sessions to reflect on what was just implemented and to plan the next session accordingly. Checklists can also be used by supervisors to provide feedback to trainees administering PFC.

Evaluating Parent Satisfaction

There is a Parent Satisfaction form included with each session's handouts (Appendix B), which we recommend using to monitor parents' satisfaction with the PFC program, as well as what homework they have completed. The clinician may also do a longer exit interview with families at the end of the PFC program to gain more detailed feedback.

Session 1   Understanding Your Child's Social Behaviors

1 Clinician and Parent Introductions

Section goal: Orient parents to purpose of Parental Friendship Coaching (PFC). Build relationships between the clinician and parents. Watch out for: Poor credibility or expectancies about treatment, barriers to alliance.

As way of introduction, the clinician can share a bit about their own background and experience with attention-deficit/hyperactivity disorder (ADHD), as appropriate. If not already done, the clinician can review the parent's social concerns about their child and explain why the PFC program may be useful for these concerns.

The clinician can then provide a bit of background of PFC. "Parental Friendship Coaching, or PFC, has been running since 2006 in several research trials. Parents have been excited about the program and have reported that it has helped their family. I hope it will be the same this time and that it will meet you and your child's needs. The goal of PFC is to help parents of children with ADHD to learn how they can improve their child's friendship-making and social skills with peers."

"Why work with parents? Historically, therapists have tried to help children with ADHD by teaching the children social skills in a therapy session. However, there's more and more evidence lately that while this helps children learn skills they do not know, this type of intervention is less successful in supporting children to actually use these skills outside of the session in real time. Researchers think this is because children with ADHD forget the skills they have learned when they are in the heat of the moment or when they are distracted by peers. But, parents can increase the likelihood that children with ADHD will show the skills they have learned in real-life peer situations, because parents can be there to remind the child with ADHD about the skills. Parents can do this until eventually, these skills become more natural and automatic for children."

DOI: 10.4324/9781003221715-3

Handout 1.1: *The PFC Pyramid*

"In this program, the first thing we work on is helping you to give your child feedback in such a way that your child will be receptive to it. We do this first because everything else relies on your child being able to take in your guidance and not be defensive about it. The second thing we target is how you can teach your child social skills that your child can use in real-life peer situations to make and keep friends. Finally, we will help you arrange good peer situations where your child can practice these social skills and where you can remind your child about the social skills in real time."

"Why work on friendship? Common sense tells us that friendship is important! Research shows that having high-quality, stable friendships improves the likelihood that children will stay in school, get better grades, and be happier and healthier. Good friendships in childhood also serve as practice for more complex relationships with romantic partners and co-workers as adults. Friendship is a skill just like any other skill such as learning to play a sport or a musical instrument. It takes practice, and practice will make your child better at it over time."

Handout 1.2: *Outline of Topics*

Review schedule of PFC topics. "This gives us a sense of what we will be covering in the PFC program, and when we will be doing it."

"For parents to get the most out of PFC, I invite you to actively participate in the program. This means thinking about each of the skills we go over, letting me know when you are skeptical about them (and it's ok if you are), and being willing to try new things even if you aren't sure if they will work."

"The PFC program is based on a lot of research about ADHD and friendship-making, but you are the expert in parenting your child and in your child's unique needs. I will present the skills that are thought to be effective based on the research, but I hope that you will also share ideas about how to best tailor these skills to fit your child. Sometimes we will have to put our heads together to troubleshoot how the skills can be adapted to fit your family situation. Any questions so far?"

Notes for Group Format

If conducting PFC in a group format, it can be useful for the clinician to prepare signs with each parent's first name, child's first name, and child's age and give them to parents as they enter. The clinician can collect the signs at the end of each session, store them, and bring them out at the beginning of each subsequent group session. The clinician can also spend time having the parents go around the room and introducing themselves and their children.

The clinician may want to mention to the group that "all parents here have children who have ADHD and who have some friendship problems," to aid group cohesion.

Consider adding meeting dates on the outline of topics (Handout 1.2).

The clinician may also want to state something like "I want parents to feel safe and share what matters to them and their child in this group. I will keep everything said within the group confidential, and I'd like to ask you to do the same. Like they say, 'what happens in Vegas stays in Vegas'; what happens in group also needs to stay in group. If you talk about this group to someone else, please focus on what you or doing for your child, instead of what other parents have said. If two group members run into each other at a social event, consider that the other parent may not want others to know that they are attending this group. By the way, if I see any of you in the community, I will not go up to you in case it would be awkward for you to have to explain how you know me; but if you want to come up to me and say hello, I am happy for you to do that."

2 Thinking about Your Child's Social Problems

Section goal: Helping the clinician get to know the child, and helping parents recognize their child's social issues. Watch out for: Parents who haven't had an opportunity to feel heard about their concerns, or who have many concerns.

"Most children with ADHD have some sort of problems getting along with peers. They may receive other treatments for their ADHD, but they still have trouble with peer relationships. Difficulties with peers can mean different things for different kids. Here is a handout that lists some common social behaviors in children with ADHD."

Handout 1.3: *Common Social Behaviors Displayed by Children with ADHD*

Go over the handout with parents, and invite them to reflect on their child's social profile. A good question to ask parents is, "which of these behaviors concerns you the most right now, and why?" This information can help the clinician know which behaviors to target. To the extent that parents raise issues that will be covered in the PFC program, say so. The clinician can also ask parents to talk more about their child's social strengths and what situations elicit those strengths. This information can help the clinician generate strategies for increasing positive social behaviors in the child. The clinician might thank parents for this information and let them know how they plan to use the information in treatment planning.

Notes for Group Format

When discussing the handout, the clinician could poll parents to indicate, with a show of hands, how many think their child shows inattentive social problems, hyperactive/impulsive social problems, and other problems. Parents could go around the room and briefly state: (a) What their primary concern is about their child's social behaviors; and (b) one thing about their child's social style that they would NOT want to change. As parents speak, the clinician can note the range of problems as well as similarities and differences between them. This can help parents to feel connected with one another. Issues to potentially consider are the child's age, gender, ADHD presentation, other comorbidities, and cultural background. Try to encourage a socially supportive environment among parents where they see each other as resources and as on the same team.

3 Antecedents, Behavior, Consequences (ABC) Model

Section goal: Introducing the concept that the child's friendship behavior can be affected by antecedents and consequences provided by the parent; antecedents are typically underused. Watch out for: Some parents may immediately say "I do all that already" or have a hard time with the idea that their behaviors can affect the child (this may feel stigmatizing).

"Most parents don't spend much effort thinking about how to help their children make friends, and this works if they have a kid without behavior problems. They tell their kid to 'go play outside,' or they sign their child up for an activity and their child makes friends, doesn't get into trouble, comes home on time, and still has time to do their homework after that." (Some parents may laugh as this is not their experience).

"But parents of kids with ADHD have to be super parents. You have to be proactive, organized, structured, consistent, and explicit with your kids if you want your kids to behave well and to make friends. We know from research that ADHD is caused by biological factors and not caused by parenting. But super-parenting is needed to help support kids with ADHD, like giving glasses to a nearsighted child is needed to help the child see even if the glasses have nothing to do with causing the child to be nearsighted to begin with."

If not already known, find out if the parent has attended behavioral parent training classes in the past. As mentioned in the Introduction to this clinical guide, we recommend the PFC program for families who have had previous experience with psychosocial treatment and are not new to the ADHD diagnosis. In particular, having been exposed to behavioral parent training will help the parent contextualize the PFC skills.

If the parent has experience with behavioral parent training, ask if they have heard of the Antecedents, Behavior, Consequences (ABC) model and if so, what (if anything) they remember about it. This is a model that is presented in behavioral parent training.

"The ABC model is a basic model of shaping child behavior that we will go back to over and over to discuss how you can encourage your child's friendships. An antecedent is something that happens before a behavior—such as moods, environmental cues, or instruction from parents that lead to a child behaving a certain way. The behavior that your child does comes in the middle. A consequence is something that happens after a behavior. The consequence can either encourage or discourage your child from behaving the same way again."

Example 1: You are at the supermarket with your child.
   Antecedent: Your child is hungry and tired already.
   Behavior: Your child throws a tantrum at the market.
   Consequence: You leave the market before your shopping is done.

Discuss: "How could you change the antecedent to reduce the likelihood that your child will show that behavior? How could you change the consequence to reduce the likelihood that your child will show this behavior again next time?" Some ideas:

- (Antecedents) Don't take your child; make sure they're not hungry and tired before going; talk to your child before you go in.
- (Consequences) Punish your child after for the tantrum; talk to your child about why that was unacceptable behavior.

"There is not one right answer or one strategy that will work every time. If there was, then all parents would know that strategy and would be doing it already, and there would be no more behavior problems in children. The point of PFC is to give parents a larger box of tools to draw upon in handling their child's behavior, specifically their social behavior with peers."

For the next example, the clinician is encouraged to select a behavior that is relevant to the parent, based on what the parent has said about the types of social problems their child has. However, two possibilities are below. Brainstorm with the parent about how to introduce antecedents that will prevent the behavior from happening, or consequences that will reduce the likelihood that the behavior will happen again, for the chosen scenario.

Example 2: Your child has a peer over to play.
   Antecedent: ?
   Behavior: Your child ignores the peer and goes off to do something alone.
   Consequence: ?

Example 3: Your child has a peer over to play.
   Antecedent:?
   Behavior: Your child gets angry because the peer is touching your child's model figurines.
   Consequence: ?

"Most parents have an easier time identifying consequences than antecedents. Consequences are necessary sometimes, but most parents don't use antecedents enough to prevent behavior problems from happening in the first place. Changing antecedents is something we will be trying to do more of. Why do you think it can be harder to focus on antecedents as opposed to consequences?" Some ideas:

- It's easier to react than to plan.
- Antecedents take effort when parents want to relax.

"However, even though they are sometimes more difficult, addressing antecedents usually pays off in the long term because this stops big problems before they happen."

Handout 1.4*: The Antecedents, Behavior, Consequences Model Worksheet*

Homework 1.1: Complete Handout 1.4. "Observe your child in a social interaction and start thinking about one antecedent and one consequence that can be reinforcing the behavior. Bring the handout back next session."

Notes for Group Format
One option is to pair parents and have them work through an ABC example with each other, so as to help more parents participate. When possible, we recommend that clinicians encourage parents to offer suggestions to each other as opposed to the clinician providing the answers (as time permits), to help parents become resources for one another in the group.

4 Special Time

Section goal: Special Time is an antecedent that will help children be more receptive to parental coaching about appropriate social behavior. Watch out for: Parents thinking Special Time sounds easy (or stupid). Parents getting impatient because they think they are not learning to address problem behavior (not understanding that Special Time is an antecedent to prevent problem behavior from occurring).

"Do you ever have the experience where you try to give guidance to your child, and the guidance is for your child's own good, and yet your child won't listen? This situation is common for parents of children with ADHD."

"Before parents can start being an effective friendship coach for their children, they first need to have a really good relationship with their child. A positive parent–child relationship is an antecedent to raise the likelihood that the parent will be able to guide their child." Remind parents what an antecedent is if needed.

"Ever noticed that the teachers/coaches who could best influence your behavior were the ones with whom you had a positive, close relationship? How did they show you that they cared about you?" Allow parents to reflect on the behaviors that these teachers/coaches showed.

"On the other hand, did you ever have a boss where it just seemed that nothing you ever did could please them and that they had to find something to criticize with everything? How motivated were you to change your behavior and accept your boss' criticism and feedback, even if there was value in that feedback?" Allow parents to reflect on how they felt in this situation.

"Children are like adults in this way! Your relationship with your child can encourage your child to listen to you and accept your guidance. I know that you already have many positive moments with your child, but I also know this is harder to maintain when children have ADHD, so there is a technique to strengthen your relationship further."

"This technique is called Special Time. Special Time has been widely used and well-validated as effective for families in general, and specifically for families of children with ADHD. There was a study where researchers had parents ask their child with ADHD to clean up a pile of trash that the child did not create. As you can imagine, children did not like this. If the parent had just done 5 minutes of Special Time immediately beforehand, the child was more likely to pick up the trash without complaining." Note to clinicians, see:

Parpal, M., & Maccoby, E. E. (1985). Maternal responsiveness and subsequent child compliance. *Child Development, 56*(5), 1326–1334.

"Special Time can be thought of as 'money in the bank'—in that with children who have ADHD, it is inevitable that parents have to correct their behavior a lot and tell them what they should not be doing. If you can build in some time where your child gets to take the lead and you are supportive of (just about) everything your child is doing, then this will make your child more compliant and better able to listen later when you need to correct their behavior. You will learn about how to correct your child starting in Session 3 of this program."

"You might wonder why Special Time is important, and other parents have initially also wondered or been skeptical at first; however, they have found it to be quite valuable, and often times the technique they appreciated the most."

Handout 1.5: *Special Time*

Go over Handout 1.5. This is a text dense handout so we recommend hitting the high points on the handout for 1–2 minutes. Instead of reading the handout, it is better for parents to learn by doing in the role-plays.

High points of Handout 1.5:

- This is a time for the parent and child to bond and have fun together.
- Just 10–15 minutes two to three times per week is enough to show an effect.
- The parent lets the child take the lead, teach the parent something, or do something the child enjoys without teaching, correcting, or dominating.
- The parent should show interest in whatever the child is interested in.

Some examples of Special Time:

- Child wants to draw and parent spends time narrating what the child is drawing. If the child wants the parent to help, the parent does the drawing the way the child wants.
- Child and parent are decorating cookies together. Parent relishes in child's creativity on the cookies and asks child to explain what they are doing. Parent refrains from telling the child how to decorate the cookies.
- Child shows parent their favorite Magic cards, and the child explains the game to the parent. Parent shows interest in this topic and listens with curiosity, even though it would not normally be interesting to them.

Parents should watch out for:

- Feeling awkward at first and then wanting to fill every space with conversation. Relax! Some silent moments are ok!
- Feeling like they are wasting possible moments to teach or correct the child. This is why Special Time is only 15 minutes!
- Needing to stop the child from doing something unsafe or harmful. If this occurs, the parent should stop the child, but it probably means that the activity was not a good one for Special Time.

This might be a good time to check in with parents about their initial impressions about (or skepticism about) Special Time, what questions they have, and how they think their child might respond.

Introduce role-plays: "Role-plays can be hard because it is putting someone on the spot, but in PFC, there are lots of role-plays so it will get better over time. We do role-plays because even if it is awkward and anxiety provoking, people learn best by doing, trying, and actively practicing. It takes courage, especially at first. I am not here to judge you, I promise!"

Role-Play 1.1: Special Time Example 1. The clinician can take the "parent" role in this first role-play and ask the parent to act like their own child in the "child" role. Try to act out a situation that is relevant for the parent. If the parent is concerned about their child responding a certain way to Special Time, then role-play that response. Afterward, ask for feedback from the parent playing the child role. Were they having fun and did they feel like the clinician playing the parent was listening?

Role-Play 1.2: Special Time Example 2. This time, encourage the parent to take the parent role, while the clinician becomes the child, for a different Special Time activity.

When debriefing after the role-play, consider that many parents will be self-conscious and focused on their mistakes. We recommend that the clinician jump in quickly with specific positive things that they saw the parent doing. For instance, clinicians could say (if true) "your positive, upbeat tone of voice really communicates interest in your child," or "nice job staying relaxed and sticking with Special Time even when your child wasn't saying much." The clinician should be hesitant about offering any negative feedback of any type at this stage, and instead bring up positive things the parent did in the role-play to reinforce them.

"Regarding Special Time, parents sometimes ask whether they should tell their child what they are doing or not. For some parents, it has worked to tell their child 'I am taking a class, and we have homework just like you do. My homework this week is to make a Special Time with you where it's just time for the two of us to do something fun. What do you think we should do?' Other parents find it better to wait for the right moment when their child is already playing and ask, 'Is it ok with you if I sit with you for a bit while you play that?'"

Homework 1.2: Special Time Practice. "Try to find 10–15 minutes two or three times this week to do Special Time with your child. For some families, it is easier to do one longer activity that is 45 minutes once per week. Generally speaking though, more times per week (even if a shorter amount for each time) is better than one longer activity."

Check in with the parent about when they expect to do Special Time, how they intend to approach it with their child, and what they imagine their child would like to do. This is a good opportunity to talk about any concerns the parent might have or troubleshoot any anticipated difficulties that have not yet been voiced. We recommend this to help improve the likelihood that the parent will be able to carry out the homework.

Notes for Group Format

Role-plays are sometimes more anxiety provoking for parents in group format because they are being watched by an audience. The clinician can acknowledge this anxiety, and remind members to be supportive, and that we are all in this together.

Usually for the first role-play, there is a parent or two who is more comfortable participating. We recommend letting the more comfortable parents do the role-plays in this session, but to suggest to parents that everyone should take a turn eventually. Consider ways to bring less comfortable parents into role-plays in future sessions, for example, by strategically identifying who should do a role-play next and by getting the buy-in of these targeted parents before the next session.

When debriefing after the role-play, the clinician should immediately ask other group members to comment on positive things they observed the role-play participants doing. This will help prime group members to be supportive to each other (and to give specific praise) after each role-play (and later, after the video recording reviews). We want parents to learn from the role-play and to have a positive experience. The clinician should be prepared to jump in with specific praise to supplement whatever the parents say (or to model this skill). For example, if a parent in the group offers the feedback "you did well not getting flustered when your child said they were bored," the clinician could add "great observation—yes I also noticed that when your child said they were bored, you acknowledged it and let them change the game, which is showing acceptance of your child and letting them take the lead."

5 Ending Business

Every session I will be asking you to do some home practices, or home-work, to try the skills at home with your child. This is intended to help translate what we are talking about in session to your day-to-day life and to helping your child. I know it can be difficult to remember to do homework or to fit it in, but I am asking you to try it because I think it is key to getting the most out of this program.

Distribute the Homework List. "We have a sheet like this every session so parents can be reminded of what their homework is. I will check in about the homework at the beginning of the next session." Parents take this Homework List home with them.

It can be useful at this point to ask the parent for feedback about how the PFC program seems to be going for them so far, what thoughts they might have about how it is fitting (or not fitting) their family's needs, and what (if anything) might improve their experience in the next session. There is also an optional Parent Satisfaction form that can be used to gather this type of feedback. Parents can complete this Parent Satisfaction form and hand it to the clinician before they leave. In future sessions, the Parent Satisfaction form will have a checklist on it where parents report what homework they have done.

Notes for Group Format
In a group format, it can be harder to check in with every parent about their experience, so the Parent Satisfaction form may be more helpful than it is in individual sessions. The clinician might say, "This is a big group, so we have a way for you to write your questions down that you may not have been able to get out in the meeting, and I will respond to them. Also, your suggestions help me to improve the group for future parents. I will be doing this every week." Consider following up individually with any parent who provided a low rating (4 or below) to better understand their concerns.

Session 2   Giving Effective Feedback to Your Child about Social Behaviors

1 Review of Homework

Section goal: To help parents identify antecedents and consequences for problematic social behaviors in their child. To troubleshoot issues with Special Time. Watch out for: Parents who have many concerns; homework review getting off topic.

Introduce homework reviews. "I want to check in about homework every week, but there is also new material to go over, so I will try to strike a balance between the two. My intention is to keep the homework review brief and move us along, but do let me know how this is for you and if the pace is not working."

Pull out Handout 1.4 that parents were asked to complete for homework. Ask if parents noticed anything about their child's social behaviors that they hadn't been aware of before. This information can be useful for the clinician to know what topics to emphasize in future sessions. Brainstorm with parents about how to change potential antecedents and consequences for behaviors.

Go over the Special Time homework assignment. Questions that may get discussion going:

- What activity did you choose?
- How did it go?
- How did your child react to the Special Time?
- Did you enjoy yourself?
- Was it hard to be positive during the Special Time?
- Was it hard to let your child take the lead?
- Were there any moments that you felt tempted to teach your child?
- Is there anything you would do differently next time?

Notes for Group Format
In a group format, the clinician may find this first homework review challenging in terms of the balance between listening to parents and not letting this part take up time allotted to the rest of the session. Sometimes in a

DOI: 10.4324/9781003221715-4

group there is one parent who has a lot they want to share (or a lot of concerns they want to discuss), and this creates a dilemma to know how to attend to this parent but also make space for other parents.

One thing we have found useful is to start an informal homework review with parents about homework as they are coming into session. This way the clinician has a sense, by the time group starts, about common issues in the homework. The clinician also has a chance to touch base with more parents without taking up official group time.

Alternatively, clinicians could do a quick poll with a show of hands at the beginning of the homework review to get a big picture (e.g., how many of you were able to do the homework this week, how many experienced some success, how many experienced some challenges). Doing so gives the clinician a preview of homework implementation. The clinician could then follow-up asking 1–2 examples of homework completion (or incompletion), success examples, and barriers faced from different parents, without having to go over detailed examples with each parent.

The clinician can always communicate that they are very interested in what parents have to say, but they also have a lot of content to go through, and ask if it is okay to move on for now. The clinician can check in 5 or 10 minutes before the end of the group to see if the parents want to go back to any of the homework topics.

2 How to Listen so Kids Will Talk

Section goal: To give parents another tool besides Special Time for relationship-building (antecedents to make it more likely that the child will accept parental coaching) and for helping the parent to understand the child's social concerns and experiences. Watch out for: Parents being concerned that active listening communicates acceptance of their child's bad behavior.

"Recall that right now we are working on ways to help your child be more receptive to your feedback. We do this so that next, when you start teaching them social skills, they are more likely to be responsive to your teaching and nondefensive about it" (refer to Handout 1.1 with the PFC Pyramid).

"We have already talked about the idea that it is easier for children to listen to their parents' instructions and guidance when they first have a very good relationship with the parent. Recall that a positive parent–child relationship is an antecedent for parents to be able to be effective friendship coaches and instruct their child so that their child will listen to them. It's like having the boss who you really like—you are more likely to accept suggestions from that boss about how to improve yourself."

"We discussed Special Time as a way to use fun activities and play to help build (or continue to make stronger) this type of positive relationship with your child. Now we are going to discuss a verbal technique that you can use to better understand your child's perspective: active listening."

"Essentially, active listening is listening to your child without responding with teaching, suggestions, too many questions, or criticism. It's good for two reasons. First, it can help parents learn more about their child's social concerns. This is helpful because you need to know what is going on before you know where to intervene. Second, it can help children be more receptive to their parents' coaching when you do make suggestions about how to help them. When your child feels like you are listening to them, your child is more likely to listen to you."

"With regard to children's social issues, parents usually express two types of hurdles." Ask parents if they relate to either of these two problems:

> #1. The child is naturally not talkative about feelings regarding peers, and this is just the way the child is.

For parents who think their child fits problem #1, "If you have a child like this, active listening can be good to try at a relaxed time when there aren't problems or stress going on. The goal is to use active listening to help your child share more about their social world with you over time. Our suggestion is to try some of these strategies slowly and see if your child will open up more, but don't push this too hard all at once. If your child doesn't open up, don't get upset; just let it go and try again the next day. If your child opens up a little bit, be sure to take interest and try not to judge or criticize, unless your child is doing something immediately dangerous. Remember how reluctant you were to admit something to a boss or parent if you thought all they would do is tell you that you should have acted differently? Finally, understand that your child perhaps will never be gushing about their emotions. This may just be how your child is."

> #2. The child is unaware of why they have problems with peers and will blame other kids, complain, and whine, without considering their own contribution to the problem.

For parents who experience problem #2: "If you have a child like this, active listening is often really helpful when your child is upset about something, such as a peer problem, or something that happened at school. Your first instinct may be to try to teach, correct, and sort out what happened. But I am saying to try to hold off on that initially, just for a bit, and try to use active listening first. I am not saying there is no time for teaching or correcting your child. You just want to be sure to listen first. When your child first feels like you have listened and you are on their side, then you will be in a better position even 10 minutes later to give your child suggestions about what they could do differently next time."

Handout 2.1: *How to Listen so Kids Will Talk*

"The first part of this handout is about opening a dialogue with your child about their friendships and social concerns. This may be most relevant to parents who experience problem #1. Good times to open the discussion are private times where parent and child are able to focus on talking without distractions or annoyances. The handout has suggestions from parents about when to have this discussion. Conversation openers are nonjudgmental statements that imply (with tone of voice and body language) that the parent cares about what has happened and wants to listen."

"The second part of the handout focuses on the content of the conversation itself. This is sometimes the hardest for parents to remember if they have a child with problem #2, or when they are confronted with a child who is upset about something that has just happened or who comes home from school after having gotten in trouble. The goal of the conversation is to focus on your child's feelings while resisting the urge to correct or teach (at least momentarily). These strategies are also used in Special Time. It's listening without judgment."

The following are the main points of Handout 2.1:
Make reflective statements

- It sounds like that really upset you.
- You've been thinking about that a lot, huh.
- You are pretty discouraged about this.
- Things are very stressful with your friend.

Make empathetic statements

- That must have been hard.
- That sounds tough.
- I'm sorry she made you so upset.

It works for some parents to offer: "Could you use a hug?"
Avoid giving solutions (for now)

- (don't say) Why don't you go say you're sorry?
- (don't say) You should tell the teacher about that.

Avoid interrupting, teaching, persuading, or confronting.
Avoid judging

- (don't say) I know you think they were being mean, but maybe they weren't.
- (don't say) I think they probably didn't like it when you told them how to play.

Avoid asking too many questions about exactly what who did what. This can feel like a police interrogation or an inquisition. Instead, ask questions about the child's feelings.

- You seemed really upset about that, can you tell me more?
- Anything else that happened with your friend today that made you upset?

Parents sometimes express that they are not okay with letting their child complain without stepping in and telling their child how to do it better. Some parents may hesitate to bring up their skepticism unless asked directly. The clinician could say something like, "I am not advocating that you never do problem-solving or give your child corrective feedback, I am just saying to not rush through the active listening part first. In most cases if the negative incident is already over and the child is upset about it, nothing will be gained by giving the child corrective feedback now as opposed to 10 minutes from now—the incident is already passed. Try to listen first to get your child to calm down and to help them feel heard. Then, your child will be more receptive to your suggestions for improvement. In other words, let's first connect with the child (with active listening), and then wait a bit and redirect to possible solutions and corrections."

"Active listening is most useful when the negative incident is already over and acting immediately, as opposed to in a little bit, won't make a difference. If your child is about to run into the street, yell 'stop!' and don't worry about letting your child take the lead or validating their feelings. Here is a situation where you taking an immediate action is necessary to prevent a very bad potential outcome."

If parents say their child will go on ad infinitum if given the chance (e.g., hours and hours): "Ironically, if you listen more, it may help kids whine less in the future. But don't expect instant results. It's okay for you to take a break and tell your child you would like to talk more about this later. You can take a break (still without giving suggestions for behavior change yet), let you and your child cool off, and then come back to it."

Role-Play 2.1: No Active Listening. The clinician might do a "bad" but realistic role-play. Say that despite our best intentions, we have all been there. Have the parent play the "child" role who should come in sort of upset and the clinician who is in the "parent" role should, with good intentions, try to correct and teach the child about what the child should have done differently. The child should respond accordingly, realistically, which might be starting to argue with the parent or getting defensive. The parent should get progressively more directive and controlling as they start to worry more that the child will not heed the parent's (correct) advice. It's good to do this role-play in this progressive way, because it rarely happens that parents start out yelling and screaming at their child; it usually creeps up like this one does. Afterward, discuss what went wrong, and how the "child" felt in this activity.

Role-Play 2.2: Active Listening Practice. Have parents do a better role-play of this same conversation. Ask the parent to take on the "parent" role while the clinician takes the role of the child that was acted out in the previous role-play. The parent should try to listen to the child and understand their emotions without correcting or teaching. Discuss afterward how the parent and child felt in this activity, as well as what might have been difficult about it.

If helpful, encourage parents to do the role-plays by:

- Stressing that we learn by doing
- Validating the anxiety parents face when role-playing
- Having the parent act out the situation that is most directly relevant to their child
- Offering specific praise regarding what the parent doing the role-play did well
- Being very judicious about giving any negative feedback

Homework 2.1: Practice Active Listening. "Try to use more active listening skills with your child at least once. You might be able to build it into Special Time."

Ask parents when they think they might try active listening. Consider asking parents what concerns they have about doing active listening, or what barriers they think they might face.

Notes for Group Format

Sometimes it helps to get more parents into discussions (without taking too much time) by asking parents in the group to indicate, with a show of hands, what applies to their child. For example, in this section, this could be done when asking parents if problem #1 or problem #2 fits their child.

It could also be useful to pair parents with each other for the second active listening role-play, if parents are reluctant to be "on stage" in front of everyone. This has the additional benefit of allowing more parents to participate in the role-play.

3 Using Praise and Corrective Feedback, Part 1

Section goal: Parents should ideally strive for a 4:1 positive to negative feedback ratio. To get this ratio, parents may need to start praising for "30% correct." Watch out for: Parents who think that praising for "30% correct" or praising 4:1 when the child's behavior is poor is loosening their standards. Some parents may have a philosophical opposition to praising (particularly for things they think their child should be doing already), or it may be difficult for them to praise because of their own upbringing.

"We are now going to start discussing specific ways to give guidance to your child in a manner that increases the probability that they will listen to you. This is still part of the base of the PFC Pyramid (see Handout 1.1)."

"In order to get children to behave more appropriately, there are two important parts: praise for skillful behaviors and corrections for negative behaviors. Both are essential. Today, we'll be talking about praise, and in the next session, we'll be talking about corrections."

"It is human nature to forget the praise because it's easier to think 'thank goodness my child is finally doing something right and I can get a moment's rest.' But, if you forget the praise you are missing a good opportunity to teach your child."

Ask parents why they think praise is a good way to guide children. Some ideas:

- When you praise a behavior, children are more likely to do the same behavior next time.
- Children like to hear praise. Children are less resistant to hearing about what they should keep doing well relative to what they should change.
- Praise is "catching." When children receive praise over time, they will be more likely to give praise, encouragement, and compliments to their peers.
- Praise, like Special Time, is "money in the bank" so that later when you have to correct your child's behavior, your child will be more receptive to listening to you because you will have built up positive interactions with your child.

"There's an amount that I am going to recommend that you praise your child. I want you to know that most parents think this sounds like an awfully large amount and say they are doing nothing close to this. Based on research, it has been found that people need a 4:1 ratio of positive-to-negative interactions to feel happy (in their marriage, in their jobs, in life). We are going to encourage you to shoot for this ratio with your children." Note to clinicians, see:

Gottman, J. M. (1994). *What predicts divorce? The relationship between marital processes and marital outcomes.* Lawrence Erlbaum Associates, Inc.

"Are you thinking that this sounds like a huge amount? Sometimes parents also say that their child doesn't have much good behavior to praise, so this would be challenging." The clinician can validate these feelings as natural and realistic for parents of kids with ADHD to have.

"Remember that the positive interactions don't always have to be praise. Special Time or active listening, or just having fun with your child, also count. But praise is another good way to build up that ratio."

"If your child doesn't have much good behavior to praise, you may need to become a 'hunter of small and often well-hidden treasures'. If your child is really far away from where you want them to be, you may need to praise when your child comes closer to desired behavior as opposed to only when your child perfectly achieves that behavior. Sometimes I say to start by praising for 30% correct. You don't have to imply to your child that everything is perfect. Just praise the specific part that your child did that is correct, even if it is only a small part of the overall behavior. As time goes on, you can progressively raise the bar. In the beginning, at least, this will allow you to maintain the 4:1 ratio."

"Remember that good social skills take time and practice (just like learning a new sport, or learning to play a musical instrument, or learning to read). This will take effort, and your child will have setbacks. Be patient with your child and with yourself."

Handout 2.2: *Giving Effective Praise to Children*

"Although praise can be used for all types of behavior, the examples on this sheet focus on behaviors with friends."

The clinician could ask parents what the difference is between the "effective" and "ineffective" examples, as a way to keep parents engaged.

The following are the main points on Handout 2.2:

- Praise more!
- If your child will get embarrassed, do it in private.
- Be specific about what you liked so the child knows exactly what to repeat.
- Don't "spoil" a good praise by adding a secret criticism. This is like someone saying to you after you got your hair cut, "oh thank goodness, that looks so much better."

This may be a good time to ask if parents feel uncomfortable with the idea of praising for children getting closer to desired behavior as opposed to achieving desired behavior, since many parents will not say so unless you specifically ask them. If so, here are some ideas that might help:

- Pick your battles. For behavior that is against the morals of your family, stay strong about not allowing this. But think about the smaller things where you might be able to relax.
- It is not motivating to the child when the child only hears criticism and when the standards for success are far beyond what the child is doing currently. Again, remember what it is like to have a boss who only finds fault with your work and who has unattainable standards.
- If you start by praising for 30% correct, you can then move the standards progressively higher as the child improves.

At the end of Handout 2.2 are 99 ways to say "good job." The clinician could ask parents to circle the ones that they could see using with their child. This may increase the likelihood that parents will try out giving more praise.

Role-Play 2.3: Praise Practice. The clinician and a parent role-play being two children interacting, such as playing a game together. The clinician should explain that we are not going to intervene during the interaction in this role-play—"Later on, we will be going over when and how you should intervene if you see negative social behavior in your child." The clinician can play the role of the parent's child but should show a range of both positive and negative social behaviors that the child would realistically do, while the other "child" in the role-play responds. After the two "children" are done playing, ask the parent to give praise to the clinician playing their child for any positive behaviors they saw.

Discuss the role-play. The clinician might ask the parent about how it felt to give the praise, and how they think their child would receive it. At this stage, we have found that most parents are still anxious about receiving negative evaluative feedback from the clinician, so we tend to still focus nearly exclusively, if not entirely, on giving specific praise to the parent about what they are doing well in the role-play, to reinforce those behaviors. It is also good modeling for the parent to learn how to do this with their child. The 4:1 praise-to-corrections ratio that we teach the parents to do with their children should apply to us as clinicians too in the feedback we are giving to parents.

Skip if not an issue: Some parents may report that their child is embarrassed by praise or doesn't seem to care about it. Most children do like praise even if they do not show it. If the child seems embarrassed, the parent can praise in private (away from other kids or adults) and state the praise to the child in one sentence, smile, and then move on to a different topic. Even if the child makes no response, the parent should watch to see if the child changes their behavior in the future because of the praise.

Homework 2.2: Praise Practice. "Try praising your child about a social interaction or social behavior you observed. Remember that you may need to praise the part that is correct even if the rest is not correct. Try to keep it separate from your Homework 2.1 conversation—the good part about active listening is that it is supposed to be nondirective and nonevaluative (like Special Time). Kids like that; don't 'spoil' active listening by jumping in and starting to be directive and solution-oriented."

Homework 2.3: Keep up Special Time. "Keep trying Special Time. You can probably build Homework 2.1 about active listening into one of the sessions of Special Time."

Notes for Group Format

In the role-play, it may be helpful to have two parents act out the roles of the two children, and then have the remaining parents who are observing be a multi-headed super parent and give praise to any of the children using the principles. The multi-headed super parent can consult with each other (and with the clinician) before deciding what to say. Debriefing with parents about what they did well as well as any places where they got stuck may also be easier (less threatening) with a multi-headed parent team, so it does not feel like the clinician is giving evaluative feedback to just one parent.

4 Ending Business

Give out the Homework List. This is for parents to take home with them.

Check in with parents about how the session went this week and how they are feeling about the homework. Consider asking if there are ways that the clinician can support them better. Ask parents to complete the Parent Satisfaction form (optional) and collect it before parents leave. The Parent Satisfaction form includes a new section reporting on whether they have completed the homework assignments for the week. This section will be on the Parent Satisfaction form in future sessions.

Notes for Group Format

If using a group format, it may be particularly useful to have parents complete the Parent Satisfaction form to help the clinician check in with everyone.

Session 3 Helping Your Child to Choose the Right Friends

1 Review of Homework

Section goal: To reinforce active listening and Special Time as relationship-building antecedents, and praise as an effective, positive way to shape behavior. Watch out for: Homework review taking too long or getting off track.

Discuss the active listening homework. Ask parents how it went, and what they learned about their child. Troubleshoot difficult spots. Ask if it was hard to be positive and not jump in and direct. Briefly also check in about parents continuing Special Time.

Discuss the praise homework and ask parents to give an example of a time they praised. Point out where the praise is specific, framed in the positive, and easy for the child to understand what behavior to continue. Possibly, ask parents what was easy and what was difficult about this assignment.

Notes for Group Format

We have found it useful to have each parent write a praising phrase they said to their child on a whiteboard in the group room. This method of reviewing homework has the benefits of allowing parents to get out of their seats, letting all parents participate, and also reducing the chances that one person will tell a very long story—there's only so much you can write on a whiteboard.

2 Using Praise and Corrective Feedback, Part 2

Section goal: When correcting child behavior, parents should keep it matter-of-fact, make it specific to the behavior (not the child's character), and state the substitute behavior they wish to see instead. Watch out for: Most parents realize this is what they should be doing, but some could use support in enacting this in the heat of the moment.

"Last session, we discussed that giving feedback to your child to change their behavior has two parts—praise and corrections—and that both are

DOI: 10.4324/9781003221715-5

essential. In the last session, we focused on how to give effective praise, and now we are going to talk about how to give effective corrective feedback."

Handout 3.1: *Giving Effective Corrective Feedback to Children*

The clinician might ask parents what the difference is between the "effective" and the "ineffective" examples on the handout. Doing this will help keep parents actively engaged in the topic. Although giving effective corrective feedback is useful for all behaviors, the examples focus on social behaviors with friends.

The following are the main points of Handout 3.1:

- If your child will get embarrassed, try to correct behavior in private whenever possible.
- Be specific about what you did not like so your child knows exactly what they need to change. Saying "your behavior is so bad" is not useful.
- Let your child know the behavior you want to see instead. It may seem unbelievable that your child wouldn't already know, but parents are surprised sometimes.
- Be matter-of-fact, stay calm, and don't make this about your child's character.
- Don't bring up past behaviors. Stick to what just happened.

Consider the following statements, which the clinician could write on a whiteboard:

- You've left the playroom a big mess.
- Stop making your friend play only what you want.

"How could each statement be improved?" Some ideas:

- Please clean up by putting your Legos in the bin.
- Let your friend choose the next game.

These corrections are better because they offer specific instructions, plus they frame the correction by telling the child the desired behavior needed, not to stop what is unwanted.

"If the child turns around their behavior after the corrective feedback, what could you say at that point to praise your child for doing so?" Some ideas:

- You really turned it around.
- Great job following directions.
- I really appreciate how you are behaving.
- You did a nice job following my instructions.

- Thank you so much for listening.
- Wow, you are doing a great job cleaning up.
- That's it, you've got it!

The clinician might also ask parents to identify what they personally think will be the hardest about giving effective corrective feedback. This will help parents apply the skills to their personal situation and also identify barriers to implementing the skills, which the clinician can help troubleshoot. This will raise the likelihood that parents will actually be able to implement the skills in the future. A common response we have gotten from parents is "remembering to do it" or "not getting mad about misbehavior."

Homework 3.1: Praise and Corrective Feedback. "Continue to try giving more effective praise and corrective feedback to your child."

Notes for Group Format
We have found the group format to be particularly useful when parents express that they get angry when their child misbehaves, and this is a barrier for them to remember to give corrective feedback in the effective way that they should. In our experience, parents are great at supporting one another and offering tips about how to deal with this common situation. Hearing these types of tips from other parents with lived experience parenting a child with ADHD is often more helpful than hearing them from a clinician.

3 Video Recording Review (Optional)

Section goal: Illustrating skills that have been covered so far in a relevant way. Watch out for: Parents may feel uncomfortable or worried about negative evaluation.

In the introduction to this clinical guide, we explained that we recommend collecting video from parents of (a) them and their child talking about how to make and keep friends; and/or (b) the child interacting with a friend. We recommended that the parent take this video recording before PFC starts and share it with the clinician. The clinician can watch the video in advance of Session 1 to gain a better understanding of the family's needs. However, we also recommend that the clinician select parts of the video to review with the parent during sessions. This is the first video recording review in the PFC clinical guide. We encourage the clinician to think about a video clip that has a good number of skillful parent behaviors so that there are many things to praise. The clinician can also think about selecting a clip that illustrates the skills being targeted currently in PFC or that are most relevant for the parent's concerns.

It is useful to acknowledge to the parent that most people hate seeing themselves on video, and so the parent may feel uncomfortable, especially at first. The reason why video recording reviews are in this clinical guide is because some parents have said this was the most helpful aspect of the PFC program, and they actually wanted more incorporated in the sessions. Like the role-plays, even though they put parents on the spot, in the end, this is a more useful learning tool than hearing the clinician talk about something in the abstract.

Play the video so that the parent and clinician can watch it together. This can often be done off a tablet or laptop. Similar to as in the role-plays, we recommend pointing out many positive examples of the skills being put into action. The clinician may want to have identified some of these behaviors in advance when preparing the video so that the clinician is ready to jump in. As in the role-plays, remember that, especially initially, most parents are anxious about negative evaluation, so we recommend that the clinician focus completely, or nearly exclusively, on the positive things the parent is doing.

Video recording reviews are written into the PFC clinical guide on seven different occasions, but these are optional and there is always flexibility to not show a video each time it says so. If conducting PFC in individual format, the clinician can choose to show multiple clips from the same initial video, or they could ask the parent to contribute a new video for discussion when it seems like this would be useful.

Notes for Group Format
Think clinically about if there are certain parent(s) in the group who would best benefit from being brought into the spotlight in this way, especially for the first video recording review. We recommend talking to the parent about it before the session and soliciting their permission to show the video.

Because this is the first time a video is shown, clinicians can orient the group first to be supportive:

- Praise and thank the parent volunteer for being so brave and state that watching oneself on video is very difficult and makes one self-conscious at first.
- Remind the group that we are here to learn from the video and to see a good model of many of the things we are working on and also to help support this parent.

In group sessions, we have typically connected a projector to a laptop and projected the video on a screen or wall so that everyone can see and hear it.

Like in the role-plays, we recommend that before the video is shown, clinicians ask the group to pay attention to the video because afterward they will be asked to point out specific positive things after they saw in the video. This will help prime the group to be supportive and to generate praise. We also recommend that the clinician be prepared to reinforce, and elaborate on, any praising statements that group members generate.

Ideally, the clinician will want to have a chance to show videos of all the families in the group by the end of the PFC program. The number of families tended to be about six to seven in our previous group administrations of PFC, so there is some flexibility to not show a video each time it says to. It is good to start planning for when video recording reviews might occur if you will need to do this.

4 Choosing a Good Friend for a Playdate

Section goal: To help parents guide their kids in choosing a peer with whom a friendship might be developed. Watch out for: Parents may feel like this is an insurmountable challenge, or this may raise parents' anxiety about networking with other families. We address networking and stigma in a later session.

"The point of the PFC program is to teach parents how to be friendship coaches for their children. So far, we have been focusing on skills for improving your communication and relationship with your child to maximize the likelihood that your child will be able to accept your guidance. We did that first because everything else relies on your child being able to listen to you" (see Handout 1.1 with the PFC Pyramid).

"Now we will start talking about other things parents can do to help their children make friends, such as teaching your child good social skills and creating an environment where your child can practice the skills. These are Steps 2 and 3 on the PFC Pyramid."

"One important thing is that parents can help children to identify good potential friends and then eventually set up carefully designed playdates for the child with that friend. Playdates are used to build and deepen the friendship. We'll be talking about this in more detail over the next few sessions, but today we are introducing the first step—how to help your child identify a good peer with whom a friendship might be developed or deepened."

"Some children with ADHD have no friends at all. The goal here will be to select a potential peer as a starting point. Other children may have one or more friends, but the friends are not good influences, the children don't get along, or the relationship is of poor quality. The goal here will either be to improve the relationship or the behavior within that friendship, and/or to make new friends so that this first relationship can be de-emphasized. Even if your child does have one friend already who is a good influence, the goal here will be to deepen the relationship with that current friend and develop other friends in addition so that your child has more options, which is especially important if the relationship with that one friend is disrupted one day."

Ask parents which situation best fits their child:

#1. No friends at all
#2. Friends but not a good friendship
#3. One good friendship, but more would be helpful

Then, ask parents to anticipate if they were to bring up the idea of a playdate with their child. Do they think their child:

#1. Would have a peer in mind that they wanted to invite?
#2. Would have a peer to invite that the parent approves of?

The clinician can use this information to understand parents' individualized treatment goals and to tailor the session to these concerns.

Handout 3.2: *Common Mistakes Made by Children with ADHD When Choosing Friends*

This handout lists common mistakes made in choosing friends. Ask parents if they see any of these problems in their child. The clinician can spend more time on whatever problems the parent brings up and skip or skim problems that are not relevant. Suggested solutions:

- Discuss with your child why you think the friendship is not a good idea. Keep it simple. For example, "I don't like the way that she treats you and doesn't let you decide what you want to do for yourself"; "It's not okay that she doesn't listen to me."
- Use active listening to understand your child's point of view. If it's problem #1, understand why your child wants to be popular and don't be judgmental about it.
- For problem #4, if you work on improving your child's behavior and giving your child lots of praise for good behavior, #4 should partly take care of itself because your child will develop a better self-image and be getting praise and attention from other places.

Skip if not an issue: "If your child has several acquaintances but their first choice for a playdate is a bad choice, try to agree to your child's second choice, provided the second choice is mostly okay with you. Or, if your child has one friend but you do not approve of that friend, try to get your child to generate a second choice and try to go with that choice."

- You can make a pact with your child that they first have to try inviting over a new child, and then after that, if they still want to, they can invite the original choice—unless things are so bad with that original choice that you don't want your child seeing them at all.
- If you make a pact, live up to your end of the bargain if your child lives up to their end. However, it is ok to say to your child right before the playdate: "If you two can behave yourselves today, then we can invite them over again. If not, this is the last time for a while." Be specific in advance with your child about what behavior you expect.
- If you are having a hard time finding any potential friends for your child who are not bad choices, you might think about how to help your

child meet new kids. We'll talk more about how to do this in a future session.

Handout 3.3: *Qualities to Look for in a Potential Friend*

This handout presents guidance to parents about what qualities to look for in a potential friend for their child. It's important to emphasize to parents that this is a wish list of ideal characteristics in the abstract, and also with all other things being equal, but someone can be a truly good friend without having all the characteristics on this list. Furthermore, most parents will not be able to find a friend for their child who has all the characteristics on this list, and especially not right away. Parents shouldn't worry about this; they should do the best that they can for the time being. Ask parents if they are able to identify who would be a good potential friend for their child, keeping these qualities in mind, and who that peer is.

Homework 3.2: Choosing a Peer for a Playdate. "Discuss with your child who they might like to invite over for a playdate. Keep in mind what we have talked about today regarding the ideal qualities of a potential friend."

Homework 3.3: Continue Relationship-Building. "Continue Special Time, active listening, etc. The idea is that these strategies will fade more into the background as they become second nature."

Playdate Progress: "From here on out, I will be encouraging you to work on arranging playdates as opportunities for your child to practice friendship skills. It is not expected that you will have a new playdate every single week. I simply wish to encourage you to make progress toward having a playdate in a way that is realistic for your family. By the end of the sessions, the goal is for you to have hosted at least one good playdate. But every family moves at their own pace, and that is ok. Each week we will go over more skills to make playdates go well, and I am asking you to try practicing some of these skills each time you have a playdate."

"For this week, start working on arranging a playdate for your child. The skills we have learned so far are:

• With your child, discuss who you would like to invite for a playdate.

If you happen to actually have the playdate before the next session happens, or to arrange a playdate, super! It is not realistic for most parents to do this, given friends' schedules and parents' schedules. So, get as far as feels reasonable to your family."

Notes for Group Format
Parents will have different goals for their children (meeting new friends, deepening existing friendships), and children will have different issues in terms of making friends. It can be useful to acknowledge the parents who

share common goals or issues so that they can use one another as resources in future sessions.

5 Ending Business

Pass out Homework List for parents to take home with them.

Parents can fill out the Parent Satisfaction form (optional) and give it to the clinician before leaving. The Parent Satisfaction form has a place to indicate whether the parents have completed the homework from the previous week.

Notes for Group Format

The Parent Satisfaction form may be more useful if PFC is being delivered in group format, because it is harder to check in with every parent.

Session 4   Preparing for a Playdate as a Host, Part 1

1 Review of Homework

Section goal: To help parents make progress from wherever they are at in terms of identifying a potential friend for the child. Watch out for: This part taking too long and detracting from the rest of the session content.

Check in with parents about the homework to decide on a good potential friend for their child and to consider inviting that peer for a playdate. It is possible that some parents will have arranged playdates, and they will be excited about sharing this. Many (most) parents will not have done so because they are still deciding who to invite, or they decided who to invite but were not able to reach the peer yet, etc. This is all okay, and the point of the homework review is for the clinician to get a sense of where parents are at and support them in taking the next steps.

In some cases, a family may have tried to contact a peer for a playdate but has not been successful in reaching the peer or getting the peer to agree to come over. This is normal and may simply mean that the other family is busy right now. The family might consider contacting another peer in the upcoming week and trying the original peer again later (in a few weeks).

Explain to parents that "in the second half of the session today we will start talking about how to host a playdate."

If useful clinically, check in about how giving corrective feedback and praise are going, as well as active listening and Special Time.

Notes for Group Format
Parents can use this time to share success stories or helpful tips with the group about how to identify a potential friend for a playdate. Sometimes if a parent hasn't done these things yet, this information helps to support them to do these things for homework in the upcoming session.

2 How to Handle Oppositional Behavior against Parental Guidance

Section goal: To reinforce previous session content about how parents can effectively guide their children. Watch out for: Sometimes parents have

DOI: 10.4324/9781003221715-6

serious differences of opinion with their partners/co-parents about discipline, and this will come out during this section.

"We've been teaching antecedents such as Special Time and active listening which improve the chances that your child will listen to your guidance about their social behaviors. But sometimes even the best designed antecedents don't work. Argumentativeness and oppositionality toward adult instructions are common among children with ADHD. For most children (not just those with ADHD), they are more likely to argue with parents than with teachers or with other adults. You can be happy knowing that it's because your child feels comfortable with you and knows you love them no matter what. However, handling your child's oppositional behavior is important because you can't guide your child to improve friendship skills—or anything else for that matter—if you are fighting all the time. This also fits into Step 1 on the PFC Pyramid" (see Handout 1.1).

"Think about the best boss or teacher or coach you ever had. Do you have a specific person in mind?" Some questions:

- What made you able to learn from their guidance?
- How did this person earn your respect?
- How did this person show they respected you and cared about your opinion?
- How did this person manage to be caring, but still maintain authority, at the same time?

"Parents are doing the same sort of thing with their children. You want to show your child you love them while also being a strong authority figure to guide them toward learning better friendship behaviors."

Handout 4.1: *Handling Oppositional and Argumentative Behaviors in Children with ADHD*

The main points of this handout are in the headings. Ask parents which points they think they are already doing well and which ones would they like to try. Ask what barriers parents foresee to implementing these points—especially barriers to the points they would like to try but haven't yet.

Regarding the point about using humor or active listening, one good example was an amazing teacher working with a child with ADHD. The child complained, "this book is so boring!" and the teacher said "oh yes it's soooooooooooooo boring" (inflection is important here: sympathetic yet humorous) and just kept teaching. Amazingly enough, the child stopped complaining. Another way to respond would be to say more seriously and empathically, "reading can be hard, and it took me a lot of practice when I was learning too," while still continuing teaching. Important is that the teacher could have said, "you're being disrespectful" or "your behavior is not appropriate," but that probably would have led to less compliance by the child.

Regarding the section on staying firm, there is a video clip from the Simpsons, "Mt. Splashmore," which can be easily found online, and the clinician can show this clip. This is a funny example of how children bug parents repeatedly to get a reaction or get what they want.

Skip if not an issue: "Sometimes parents are not sure what type of rewards to use when making a behavior contract, or they are concerned about giving their children expensive things for doing behaviors they should be doing anyway. For some children (especially younger children), praise is enough of a reward. A space on the refrigerator where you draw smiley faces or put stickers every time your child shows the desired behavior may be enough. For children who may respond better to bigger incentives, consider inexpensive, easy things such as TV/screen time, or your child gets to choose a movie for family movie night, or your child gets a treat at dinner such as soda or a cookie (if you allow this in your house)."

Role-Play 4.1: Handling Oppositional Behavior. The parent can role-play the "parent," and the clinician can role-play the "child," trying to enact behaviors that the parent sees in their child. Ask the parent which point on the handout they would like to practice during this role-play. It could be discussing with the child the reason behind a rule, or giving a clear command, or staying calm while the child is whining, for instance.

As with the other role-plays and video recording reviews, we advise debriefing with the parent afterward by giving a lot of specific praise for the things the parent did well. At this point in the PFC program, some parents are seeking suggestions for improvement. There will be variability among parents in this, however. If it seems clinically appropriate, the clinician might turn to the parent after first giving lots of praise and then say "was there any place where you felt stuck or felt like you were struggling?" Only if the parent brings up something, brainstorm with the parent about ways to handle the difficulty. Regardless, we recommend sticking to at least a 4:1 positive-to-corrective feedback ratio in what the clinician provides to the parent.

Homework 4.1: Handling Oppositional Behavior Practice. "Experiment with trying out one of the things on the list to handle oppositional behavior. You should choose one new strategy that you think might work with your child." Parents should individualize this homework assignment to pick the strategy they want to work on.

Notes for Group Format

At this stage in group sessions, we are usually able to have two parents take part in the role-plays: one in the parent role and the other in the child role. We usually recommend this, because it gets more parents involved in the role-play.

We also encourage parents to brainstorm and troubleshoot with each other when they have concerns about how to implement the skills, as much as time allows.

3 Video Recording Review (Optional)

Section goal: Illustrating skills that have been covered so far in a relevant way. Watch out for: Parents may feel uncomfortable or worried about negative evaluation.

"Like we did last time, we will be going over another video of you with your child to demonstrate the use of effective skills (such as active listening, praise, corrective feedback, and effectively handling children's oppositional behavior)."

The clinician can pick a different portion of the video that the parent already submitted or can pick a different video entirely. During the discussion of the video with the parent, remember to point out lots of specific, positive ways that the parent is enacting PFC skills. Potentially, the clinician can ask the parent if they noticed anything new, anything that surprised them, or anything that they had questions about or wanted help with.

Notes for Group Format
The clinician will probably want to select a different parent's video from the parent shown last week. Again, the clinician should think clinically about which tape to choose based on who is showing a lot of good examples of these skills, who needs to be drawn into the group, who it might benefit the most, and who wouldn't be too self-conscious. We advise that the clinician ask permission from the parent and give the parent a heads-up in advance.

When preparing the video clip to show, we recommend that the clinician think about several specific behaviors that the parent did well to identify for the group. The clinician can state during the discussion that one reason they selected this video was that they thought the parent did a really good job displaying X skill when the parent said Y (be as specific with praise as possible). Encourage the group to give positive feedback by asking for examples of what the parent did really well.

4 Preventing Boredom and Conflict During a Playdate, Part 1

Section goal: There are antecedents that can increase the likelihood that the playdate will go well. This again is like money in the bank—spending the time on these antecedents now will prevent problems later. Watch out for: Parents feeling overwhelmed by the large number of things they are asked to do. One thing that may help is reminding parents that they are not expected to do these things forever; they are mainly important when a friendship is getting started.

"In the last session, we worked on identifying a peer as a potential friend for your child. Once you and your child have identified a peer, now you're ready to prepare to invite the peer over and to have the playdate itself. We are starting to talk about what to actually do on a playdate, and specifically, how parents can structure the playdate to increase the likelihood that the children will get along and have fun (and deepen a friendship). This falls under Steps 2 and 3 on the PFC Pyramid" (see Handout 1.1).

"The main obstacles to children having good playdates are boredom and conflict. But there are things that parents can do to minimize the likelihood that boredom and conflict will occur, through using good antecedents. If parents arrange a few antecedents, they will save time later when they prevent big problems from happening. Today, we are going to talk more about antecedents to prevent boredom, and we'll continue this conversation next session with antecedents to prevent conflict."

Ask parents to think about the last 1:1 conversation or lunch date they had where they were really bored. Ask why they were bored. Some possibilities:

- We talked about a subject I know little about.
- The other person was not doing a good job in trying to include me.
- The other person didn't seem excited or happy to see me.
- We ran out of things to talk about; we had few common interests.

"Children often get bored during playdates for the same reasons, so now we are going to talk about how parents can prevent each of these things using antecedents."

Handout 4.2: *Preventing Boredom and Conflict on Playdates*

The take-away points of Handout 4.2 are the bolded sections. The first six points are common reasons why kids get bored on playdates and some suggestions to help prevent boredom. The clinician might ask parents which points they already do and which ones they would like to work on for the next playdate.

"One important way to prevent boredom is in the way you set up the playdate before it happens.

Playdates generally go more smoothly if the children have talked with each other first about what they might want to do on the playdate. After the children confer, then the parents get involved to confirm the details of the activities the kids want to do, make sure everything is ok with both sets of parents, and plan the logistics of carrying out the activities."

"There are general steps that you can follow, once a peer has been identified that you want to invite for a playdate:"

- Ask your child what activities they might want to do with the peer.
- Consider whether the peer will find those activities fun. You and your child may not know this, especially if the peer is a new friend.

- Consider whether those activities are logistically feasible, meaning not overly expensive, not unsafe, fit the length of the playdate, fit the weather, and any materials needed are available or easy to obtain.
- Consider whether those activities are likely to bring out problem behaviors in your child like aggression or obsessiveness; if so, you probably want to consider other activities.

Ask parents how these steps match their impression of what other parents are doing. There is variability in how playdates are conducted, which could relate to neighborhood, socioeconomic status, racial/ethnic background, gender, or other cultural factors. It is important for the clinician to understand and be sensitive to these differences so that they can propose a treatment plan that fits parents' individualized needs. The word "playdate" in this clinical guide broadly applies to any social interaction between the child and peer where they have an opportunity to interact, the child can practice their positive social behaviors, and a relationship between the two children can be built or deepened. For some families, this will mean inviting the peer over for a play session at the child's home. For other families, this will mean arranging for the child and peer to meet at a park, a mall, a playground, the beach, an arcade, or a skating rink. Other families will prefer to take the child and peer for ice cream, or for pizza.

Ask parents whether they are comfortable with doing these steps, as well as any barriers they foresee in carrying out these steps.

"You and your child should identify around three potential activities for the playdate that are feasible and safe and that the child and peer are likely to find fun (to the best of your knowledge). At this point, you should coach your child to invite the peer to have a playdate and to talk to the peer about whether they want to do any of these activities. It is particularly important to do this with peers who have not had a playdate with your child before, because you and your child may not know what the peer likes to do."

"Your child might have this conversation with the peer in different ways:"

- One common way is for children to talk about it at school or wherever it is that the children see one another. A downside is that parents won't be around to supervise the conversation, but it realistically reflects what children typically do.
- If the peer lives in the neighborhood, another common way is for your child to approach the peer when they happen to see them outside; this might allow you to oversee the conversation from a distance. But your neighborhood may not be set up like this.
- Some children text or call the peer (often using the parent's phone) to have this conversation, and depending on your situation, this may be the most realistic option.

"A typical process, however, is that your child and the peer agree that they want to have a playdate and talk about what they want to do together, and your child tells you about this conversation. You then contact the parent of the peer (often by text, but sometimes by email or phone or in person) to work out the details of the playdate. For instance, you would talk to the other parent about the date and time, the meeting location, and who is doing drop-off and pickup and also arrange for the peer to bring anything needed for the activity."

"Here are some more guidelines about what to expect given your child's age:"

- Ages 6–8: Child and peer might say "let's play Beyblades" or "we could ride bikes," but do not discuss details about materials needed for these activities. The parent may need to encourage this conversation and remind the child to have it. The conversation between the children might be very brief, like one or two sentences. The children are probably not thinking about how long each activity will take. The parent considers these details and talks with the other parent to arrange everything.
- Ages 9–11: The child and peer might have longer conversations about what they will do together. They may weigh potential different activities before choosing one or two. They may also start considering when to meet up to do the activity. The parents still get involved at the end to arrange drop-off and pickup, but the decisions on activities are left increasingly to the children.

"However, many children with ADHD do not have experience with friendships and playdates, and they are functioning on the level of a child who is younger than their age. So, parents likely need to offer more support to children with ADHD in this process, especially at the beginning."

Handout 4.3: *Talking to a Peer about What to Do on a Playdate*

The following are the main points of Handout 4.3:

- Parents should first prepare the child for talking to the peer through having a discussion with their child about it, role-playing with their child, or having their child practice with someone else such as a cousin or sibling.
- Children should adopt a style called Play Detective (younger children like this term), or for older children, this style can be described simply as "finding out what the other child likes to do."
- Parents should figure out a good time and place for the child to have this conversation with the peer (e.g., at school, in the neighborhood, over texting or phone).
- After the conversation is done, parents should praise the child for carrying it out.
- Depending on if the parent was able to observe the conversation between the child and peer, the parent could give feedback to the

child about what just happened, remembering the 4:1 praise to corrections ratio.

"The Play Detective step is for children to find out more about each other and see if they have common interests that they would like to do on a playdate. Your child is like a detective—they have to solve the mystery of what the other child likes to play and what they could do together. If your child tends to fire away a bunch of questions without waiting for the answers or alternatively tends to not say anything at all, it's probably a good idea to role-play how to be a good detective with your child before they approach the peer."

Role-Play 4.2: Coaching Your Child to Talk with a Peer. The clinician plays the "child" role, and the parent plays the "parent" role. The parent coaches the child about how to have this conversation with the peer, given the context that the parent thinks will work (e.g., at school, in the neighborhood, via texting or phone). The role-play should match whatever situation the parent needs help with. In other words, if that parent's child has no problem asking the questions but has trouble listening to the peer, then the role-play should focus on that. By contrast, if that parent's child has never asked these types of questions at all, then focus on this in the role-play.

Homework 4.2: Practice Talking with a Peer about What to Do on a Playdate. "Try this at home with your child. If your child has never done this before or if you suspect this will not go well the first time around, then have a practice conversation. Talking to a cousin about the same age as your child or a sibling may be a good idea for practice. Once your child has the hang of it, the goal is for your child to try having this conversation with a peer who you have identified as a potential friend, and asking them for a playdate."

"In the past, some parents have started to feel overwhelmed about the number of things they are supposed to be doing before every playdate. I want to emphasize that these are just suggestions. While I recommend that parents try to do more of these things, it is not realistic to do all of them every time. Also, parents are not expected to do these things forever. It is probably most important to follow these suggestions in the first few playdates that your child has, because the friendship is getting started. Think about this like a 'first date' situation. Once kids have become good friends, these antecedents can be relaxed."

Playdate Progress: "I want to encourage you to continue to make progress toward hosting fun, structured playdates to help your child practice friendship skills. But I realize that each parent will be at a different stage of the process to host a playdate, because every child is different, and this also depends on friends' schedules which are out of your control."

"So far we have spent two sessions learning different strategies to make playdates go more smoothly. I'd like to encourage you to keep working on hosting a playdate and practicing these strategies. Here are the skills we have gone over:"

- With your child, discuss who you would like to invite for a playdate.
- (New Skill) Help your child talk to the friend to decide what to play.
- (New Skill) Prepare fun activities for the playdate.
- (New Skill) Ensure your child is not tired or hungry before the playdate.

Occasionally, some parents will already have invited a peer for a playdate and have set a date and time, but the playdate has not occurred yet. This is great, and the clinician should encourage the parent to have their child talk to the peer about what they want to do on the upcoming playdate. Note that if the parent already had a playdate in the past week, which is rare, they can think about arranging a new playdate and trying out some of the new skills when the next playdate occurs.

Homework 4.3: Continue Relationship-Building. "Continue Special Time, active listening, praise, etc. The idea is that these strategies will fade more into the background as they become second nature."

Skip if not an issue: "Some parents may wonder if they should allow their child and peer to decide they want to watch TV or play video games during the playdate. It depends on how your child interacts during these activities. In some peer groups (especially 8–10-year-old boys), video games are popular, and if your child and the peer have fun doing them and play well together, then it makes sense to allow these activities. Some children have problems with TV and video games because it leads to them ignoring the peer, little interaction, competitiveness, or conflict. Or, perhaps your child plays too many video games already and you would like to encourage something else. If TV and video games are a problem for your child, then make them off limits during playdates."

Skip if not an issue: Ask if parents are concerned about what to do with siblings during the playdate. "Sometimes siblings can get in the way of your child and the peer building a relationship with each other. In the past, parents with multiple kids have handled this problem by arranging two playdates at the same time, one for each sib. Or, while one child has a playdate, the sib gets to do something special that they like such as watch a video. Or, if there are two parents in the family, one parent handles the child and their playdate, while the second parent does something fun with the sib. However, this is not always practical so like all tips, I advise parents to do what works for their family."

Notes for Group Format

The role-play can be done with two parents (one in each role), instead of the parent and the clinician.

In some cases, group members have also wanted to have playdates with one another. We have never initiated this idea, but sometimes parents bring it up on their own. There is no rule against it, provided this is something the parents want to do. We encourage the parents to keep in mind the suggestions for choosing a good friend for their child, but a good friend could be the child of another group member. Some parents also feel more comfortable having a first playdate with another group member who understands their situation, especially if they are not having any playdates at the moment. So, a playdate with another group member can be a good way to get the ball rolling. However, the clinician should consider the following:

- Parents may feel left out if they are not invited for playdates by other members.
- Parents may feel pressure to accept another parent's playdate invitation, given that they are seeing each other regularly for group.
- A negative interaction may happen during the playdate and the parents carry bad feelings about it into group.

Therefore, another possibility is that the clinician might ask parents to refrain from playdates with other group members until the end of the group, after which they are encouraged to have them if they choose.

5 Ending Business

Pass out the Homework List and Parent Satisfaction form (optional). The clinician can draw parents' attention to the "Playdate Progress" section in the Parent Satisfaction forms; this section will continue for the rest of the sessions.

The Homework List is for parents to take home with them. Parents fill out the Parent Satisfaction form for that week and give it to the clinician before leaving.

Notes for Group Format
The Parent Satisfaction form may be more useful if PFC is being delivered in group format, because it is harder to check in with every parent.

Session 5   Teaching Your Child Social Skills, Part 1

1 Review of Homework

Section goal: Some parents will have their first playdates hosted or arranged, and they will be excited to share this. Watch out for: Realistically, some parents will take longer to have playdates. This is okay, and the clinician can brainstorm with them about how to get around obstacles. If they have not been able to set up a playdate with a peer because that peer has been hard to reach, they could try another peer and come back to the first one later.

"At the end of today, we are halfway through the PFC program. We hope that at this point, parents are doing well on their way toward identifying a potential friend for their child, contacting that peer, and arranging a playdate."

Review progress toward playdates and troubleshoot any issues that have arisen.

If clinically useful, review the homework about handling oppositional and argumentative behaviors.

"In terms of homework for the upcoming weeks, parents will be continuing to integrate Special Time, active listening, praise, and corrective feedback more into their weekly routine with their children. If you notice Special Time was working, and it has been falling off, you might want to make a particular effort to set up at least one Special Time this week."

Notes for Group Format

There can be a tricky balance in a group when parents are all at different stages of the playdate arrangement process. We are often thinking about how to meet parents where they are at and to help parents learn from others who may be farther along in the process but also to ensure parents do not feel bad for being less far along than others. We often try to emphasize that every family's situation is different and that the group is here to support one another.

DOI: 10.4324/9781003221715-7

2 Video Recording Review (Optional)

Section goal: Illustrating skills that have been covered so far in a relevant way. Watch out for: Parents may feel uncomfortable or worried about negative evaluation.

Similar to as in previous sessions, here is another opportunity to review video of the parent and child to demonstrate various skills that have been covered so far and to bring the material to life. If PFC is being delivered in individual format, the clinician can select another clip from a previously used tape, or at any time, the clinician can ask the parent to make a new tape. As always, give lots of specific praise for positive behaviors and debrief about the video. The parent may also bring up places where they felt unsure about what to do, or the clinician could elicit that conversation. If the parent is comfortable with it, this could be an opening to brainstorm about things the parent might want to try next time.

Notes for Group Format

Again, clinicians should think strategically about which tape to choose, ask permission from the parent, and give the parent a heads-up in advance. Show the video and encourage the group to give positive feedback by asking what the parent did really well. Ask the parent if they noticed anything new, anything that surprised them, or anything that they had questions about or wanted help with.

3 Helping Your Child Learn Good Friendship Skills, Part 1

Section goal: Children this age commonly play games with each other to make friends. Children with ADHD often need support with these skills. Watch out for: Sometimes parents are not accustomed to observing their child's play enough to know the nuances of their child's problem behavior in this context.

"In this session, we will be going over things that children with ADHD tend to do in peer interactions and on playdates that get in the way of their friendships, and how parents might help."

The clinician can remind parents of the overall philosophy of PFC. "First, we focused on helping parents help their children to be more receptive to parental feedback (Special Time, active listening, effective praise/corrective feedback, handling oppositional behavior), and lately we have moved into specific ways that parents can teach social skills and structure the environment so that the child can practice these social skills. Here is an example of an important social skill that parents can teach: game-playing skills. This is Step 2 on the PFC Pyramid (Handout 1.1)."

"When you coach your child to teach them better social skills before they go on a playdate, this is an antecedent. Importantly, parents are uniquely in a great position to teach their kids social skills! Unlike a therapist, parents have the opportunity to see their kids in action in their real social environments. Parents know their kids best and also know how they are likely to respond. Parents are also around to remind their child about good social skills in the heat of the moment."

"The first thing we will discuss is helping your child to have interests and game-playing skills that attract other children. Some children have 'interactive' interests that encourage other children to have something to play with them. But some children do not."

- Not good interactive interests: Children who would rather read by themselves than approach another child, and children who prefer pretend play that doesn't include other kids.
- Good interactive interests: Ball games or sports that other kids play, common board games with simple rules, common toys in their peer group, video game knowledge (in some peer groups).

Optional: If clinicians have some common games for school-age children in their office already, they could bring them out so parents can look at them.

"Some kids with ADHD tend to shy away from these interactive interests because they require too much patience, concentration, and memorization of rules. Parents can help these kids learn to develop these interests if they don't already have them."

"Other kids with ADHD have these interactive interests, but they don't play very skillfully. For these types of children, parents can step in to help teach their child more socially skilled game-playing behavior." For example:

- They make up their own rules to games and argue about the rules with other kids.
- They dictate the game, so they are telling everyone whose turn it is and where they should move.
- They space out, forget their turn, or forget the rules.
- They don't notice when other kids playing the game are getting bored, mad, or both.

The clinician can ask parents if they think their child has problem #1 (not having enough interactive interests/games), problem #2 (likes/knows the games but breaks the rules in ways that put off peers), or both problems. These questions can help keep parents engaged and help them apply the topic to their child. The clinician can use the answers to these questions to better understand the needs of the child and to tailor the rest of this section to those needs.

Handout 5.1: *Helping Your Child Improve Game-Playing Skills*

"Handout 5.1 contains some suggestions for how you can help your child with both types of problems by playing games with them. If the problem is that your child doesn't know enough games, this will teach them the game and the rules. If your child already knows the game but doesn't play it skillfully, then this is a chance to teach your child how to play better. As explained on Handout 5.1, you might talk to your child in advance about the problem behavior."

Have parents read the script that is on the second page of Handout 5.1 (note, it's reprinted here):

PARENT: How do you think you could tell if your friend is getting bored of the game?

CHILD: I don't know, maybe he'd be looking across the room.

PARENT: Great! Any other ideas?

CHILD: Maybe he'd seem like he wasn't excited anymore.

PARENT: I think that's exactly right. If you saw this happening, what could you do?

CHILD: Ask him if he wants to play something else.

PARENT: That sounds great. Let's practice this at our next family game night. At some point, I am going to act bored and I want to see if you can pick up on that and if you'll ask me if I want to play something else, okay?

"One parent had the problem of a child who would get upset when losing and stomp off in a tantrum. The child did this with peers and with parents. Because of that, the parents stopped playing games as a family because it was so stressful and stopped having playdates. This is a natural but wrong approach. Why do you think that is?" Some ideas:

- Without practice, the child will never learn to control disappointment when losing.

What could the parents do instead? Some ideas:

- Play with the child for real and not let the child win.
- Possibly discuss in advance that if the child can stay calm through the game, the parents will provide a reward.
- If the child is getting worked up, take a break to cool down. (Next week, we will be learning more ways you can teach your child how to handle negative emotions and calm down when upset).
- Praise the child for trying to stay calm or for any improvement in this behavior at all, even if the child doesn't do this perfectly.

Skip if not an issue: "Some children are intensely interested in one toy with too little regard for the peer. Or the interest could be TV or video games, depending on how your child tends to engage in these activities. Make a deal to reduce the interest:"

PARENT: You need to find another toy to play with for 30 minutes before you play with Barbies.

CHILD: But I don't like playing with anything else.

PARENT: You need to give your dolls a rest and give another toy a try. What's it going to be? Roller blading? Painting?

CHILD: I'll roller blade then.

PARENT: Good, roller blade for the next 30 minutes and then you can play with your Barbies.

The parent needs to enforce the minimum 30-minute limit. However, if the child wants to roller blade for longer than 30 mins, the parent can let that happen.

Skip if not an issue: "Don't let an interest exclude playmates. If your child has an interest that can exclude peers, make a deal with your child right before the playdate (this is changing the antecedents). For instance, if TV is a problem for your child because this is all your child wants to do, and they ignore peers when the TV is on:"

PARENT: When Miguel comes over, it's time to play with him, so no TV. Have Miguel help you pick a game to play.

CHILD: What if he wants to watch TV?

PARENT: If he asks, just tell him your parents don't allow TV when guests are over.

PARENT: You can play with Legos if you agree to let Leah be in charge of what you build. You have a choice to either let Leah choose what she wants to play or we'll put the Legos away until Leah leaves. What would you like to do?

CHILD: I'll let Leah pick what we do.

PARENT: Good. We'll try it. If you can't let Leah choose, then we will have to put the Legos away.

CHILD: Okay.

Role-Play 5.1: Playing a Game with Your Child. This role-play is better if the clinician has a common children's game in their office already. We have found Jenga to be useful. The clinician can play the role of the "child" and try to replicate the game-playing behaviors that the parent observes in their child. For instance, if the child needs to learn the game, then role-play that. If the problem is that the child likes to make up their own rules (or has one of the other social skills problems listed above), then role-play that instead. The parent can play the role of the "parent" and try to work on these behaviors.

At this stage in the PFC program, the clinician might work on encouraging the parent to self-monitor and be the one to suggest the things they think they did well in the role-play, or what they would like to work on for next time. The idea is that the parent is thinking about their own performance and generating the ideas, as opposed to the clinician providing an evaluation of the parent's performance. This approach may help support parents to carry out the skills in the future when the clinician is not present.

As with all role-plays (and video recording reviews), remember the guidance about how to debrief so as to encourage the parent learning (and having a good experience).

Homework 5.1: Game Skills Practice. "If the problem is that your child doesn't know or like enough games, pick a game to teach your child, borrow or buy it (if necessary), and play it with your child. If you think your child has enough game knowledge but you are concerned about their behavior when playing, then pick a game your child already knows and play it with them. Generate the situations where your child shows problems. For instance, if your child fails to notice when a peer is bored, talk to your child about this in advance and then show that you are bored at some point in the game. Use the effective ways of giving praise and corrective feedback to teach your child how to respond appropriately when you show you are bored."

"This teaching activity should be done separately from Special Time, where the child gets to dictate the rules. This is one reason why, sometimes, it is better for parents to not play board games or games with rules during Special Time."

Notes for Group Format

We have found it useful to poll parents with a show of hands to indicate which of the game-playing problems their children have. This is a quick way to get information about the relevant problems for the group members and help everyone participate.

In a group format, we also recommend having one parent play the "parent" role and another parent play the "child" role in a role-play.

4 Preventing Boredom and Conflict during a Playdate, Part 2

Section goal: To learn antecedents to prevent conflict from happening on a playdate. Watch out for: Like the antecedents to prevent boredom, these take planning and effort to implement, and parents may feel overwhelmed about the number of things they are being asked to do.

"Last week we started talking about how boredom and conflict can get in the way of playdates, and we discussed several things to prevent boredom."

- Have the children talk in advance about things they would both like to do on the playdate.
- Set up activities in advance, make sure they are structured, and arrange to have all the materials you need.

- Make sure your child is in an optimal mood (well-rested, full, and having taken their medication if this helps their social behaviors).

"These are all things that further Steps 2 and 3 on the PFC Pyramid (Handout 1.1). Today, we are going to focus more on antecedents to prevent conflict from happening. Some antecedents to prevent conflict are ones we already discussed for preventing boredom, because they help prevent both boredom and conflict."

"There are more antecedents that are specifically for preventing conflict."

- Put away toys that your child doesn't want to share. For example, if your child has spent a lot of time making a Lego model and they don't want the friend to touch it or to take it apart, then your child (with your help) should put it away for the playdate. A good place for this is the parent's bedroom.
- Talk to your child in advance before the friend comes over about how to be a good host.

Handout 5.2: *Being a Good Host*

The idea behind Handout 5.2 is that parents can go over these rules with their child in advance before the playdate. The main rules are all the ones listed in bold on the handout.

The clinician might have parents look at the handout and identify the things that they think their child is already doing well versus needs to work on. This will help keep parents involved and improve the likelihood that they will actually work on these skills with their child. In addition, this will help parents to notice things to praise in their child.

"Some parents physically show their child this handout and go through the rules together. This may be helpful because it makes the rules come from a different authority than the parent (which some children are more likely to accept). However, other parents find it less awkward to introduce the rules in a casual conversation and not bring the handout." Ask parents what they think will work best for their family.

"You should target one main rule for improvement, to start with. If you think your child is breaking all of the rules, this may be hard, but try to start with one at a time so that it is not overwhelming. Also, set a realistic goal for improvement, considering where your child is at right now. For instance, regarding rule #2, if your child is doing none of these things, then shoot for 'better.' If your child is in the 'better' column already, then shoot for 'best'."

"If you think your child is doing well (or even 50% well) on any of the rules, remember to praise for that! You can say in the discussion with your child that 'I have noticed that you do a good job with this rule.'"

Skip if not an issue:

- The exception to rule #1 is if the guest has physically hurt your child on purpose or if the guest is doing dangerous things and won't obey your instructions, then it's time to contact the guest's parents and stop the playdate. Otherwise, if the guest is bossy or rude, mostly your child should try to be polite and try to let the guest be right. You don't have to have another playdate with the guest.
- Some children, after reading rule #1, will say something like, "So if the guest is always right, does that mean that I can do whatever I like when I am at someone else's house?" The answer to this is: "If the other child is a good host, then they will allow you to for that time only, but after that they probably will not want you to come over anymore. Think about how you would feel if your guest was rude. Would you want to play with that guest anymore?"

Role-Play 5.2: Talking to Your Child about Being a Good Host. The parent could play the "parent" role, while the clinician takes the role of the "child." The parent should practice talking to the child about the "good host" rules. The parent might go through the list with the child and talk about what the child already does really well on the good host list and then pick a behavior to target, depending on the child's needs.

Playdate Progress:

"As in the past sessions, I am encouraging you to keep working on playdates. Here are the skills we have gone over:"

- With your child, discuss who you would like to invite for a playdate.
- Help your child talk to the friend to decide what to play.
- Prepare fun activities for the playdate.
- Ensure your child is not tired or hungry before the playdate.
- (New Skill) Before the playdate, talk to your child about being a good host.
- (New Skill) Put away any toys that are likely to cause conflict.

"It's better if you can manipulate the antecedents first to make the playdate go smoothly. However, if that doesn't work, there are other strategies during the playdate to stop early signs of boredom or conflict. We will be talking about how to do this next week."

Homework 5.2: Continue Relationship-Building. "Continue Special Time, active listening, praise/corrective feedback, etc."

Notes for Group Format

During this role-play, consider dividing the group into pairs of two parents so that more people can get practice, and it may take the pressure off in terms of a parent being on stage. Sometimes we have paired parents based on who is working on similar problems.

5 Ending Business

Pass out the Homework List and Parent Satisfaction form (optional). The Homework List is for parents to take home with them. Parents fill out the Parent Satisfaction form for that week and give it to the clinician before leaving.

Notes for Group Format

The Parent Satisfaction form may be more useful if PFC is being delivered in group format.

Session 6   Preparing for a Playdate as a Host, Part 2

1 Review of Homework

Section goal: More parents will have had their first playdates by this point. The goal is to go over the big picture steps toward setting up a high-quality, successful playdate. Watch out for: Making sure parents are on the right track and that any barriers can be discussed.

Check in with parents about their homework assignment to work on good game-playing skills and their progress on their playdates. Troubleshoot any issues.

Review the big picture steps about setting up a high-quality, successful playdate:

1 Choosing the right potential friend
2 Helping your child to invite the friend for a playdate
3 Preparing for the playdate to prevent boredom and conflict
4 Teaching your child good friendship skills

The clinician can write the steps on a whiteboard or a flip chart; the benefit of a flip chart is that every week from here on out, the clinician will be referring to this list of steps during homework review, so they will not need to re-write them every week.

"This week we will be working on the next step in this process, which is:"

5 Intervening in the playdate if boredom and conflict are starting to occur

Notes for Group Format
In this session, we have often found it helpful to pair parents to trouble-shoot and brainstorm with each other about playdate progress. Parents are often at a stage where they can help one another, and it may help parents who have not had playdates yet to receive the extra help they need (or to free the clinician to help those parents).

DOI: 10.4324/9781003221715-8

2 Helping Your Child Learn Good Friendship Skills, Part 2

Section goal: Helping parents identify and troubleshoot common conversational skills problems. Watch out for: Parents who have trouble prioritizing what to target, so they can be too negative as a result (not preserving 4:1 praise-to-corrections ratio).

"Last session we started learning ways that parents can teach their children social skills that will help children make and keep friends. This corresponds to Step 2 on the PFC Pyramid (Handout 1.1). The first skill we focused on last session was game-playing skills. This session we are introducing another important social skill for friendships, which is how to have conversations."

"Conversational skills are essential for deepening friendships, and something children with ADHD tend to struggle with. Conversational skills also become more important as your child gets older. Teaching your child good conversational skills, just like teaching your child good play skills, is another antecedent to encourage the peer interaction to go well."

Handout 6.1: *Common Mistakes in Conversational Skills Made by Children with ADHD*

Ask parents which mistakes on Handout 6.1. they see in their child. The clinician can use this information to get to know the child better and to understand what conversational skills to target.

Parents may have a list of several problems they see in their child's conversational skills. However, they should pick one main problem they would like to target first. As a starting point, they might use one of these guidelines to pick the behavior to target:

- The behavior that is likely to be the easiest for the child to change or improve
- The behavior that is the worst
- The behavior that has the biggest detrimental impact on their child's peer relationships
- The behavior that occurs the most often

The clinician could ask parents why they think it is recommended to only target one behavior at first. The main idea: "The rationale behind picking just one behavior to target is so that your child doesn't feel overwhelmed and so that you can more easily keep up that 4:1 ratio of praise-to-corrective feedback. Once your child masters one conversational skill, then you can move to other behaviors on the list."

Ask parents to identify the problem behavior they picked. This will help parents to personalize the activity to their child.

Handout 6.2: *Conversational Skills Worksheet*

This worksheet guides parents through the steps of how to work on the behavior that the parent picked.

Regarding antecedents, "Talk to your child about it in advance and make it clear exactly what behavior you are targeting. Try to frame the behavior in terms of what you want to see, as opposed to in terms of what you don't want to see. For example, if the child's problem is monopolizing the conversation:"

> BAD: Don't monopolize the conversation. (This is framed as a "don't" and not specific).
> BETTER: Don't talk the whole conversation without letting your friend say anything. (This is specific but still framed as a "don't.")
> EVEN BETTER: Take turns talking with your friend. If you've been talking for a while, ask your friend a question if you need to, and be quiet. (This is specific, and framed as what you want your child to do.)

"As another antecedent, you might do a role-play with your child to practice the behavior that you want your child to do, similar to the way in which we do role-plays in here for practice."

On the worksheet, if the parent suggests "talking to child about the problem" as an antecedent, have the parent come up with and write down the exact phrases that they will say. The clinician can help by checking for appropriate specificity and framing as what the parent wants the child to do.

Regarding behavior, "Then, observe your child in a peer situation to see how your child carries out the behavior you are targeting. Try to be patient with your child and with yourself; this is a learning process."

Regarding consequences, "Give your child specific, direct feedback immediately after about how they did with the conversational skill that you were working on. Find something to praise, even if it is 30% correct." Encourage parents to write on the worksheet exactly what they will say. The clinician can evaluate how the phrase follows the principles of effective praise and corrective feedback discussed in PFC Sessions 2 and 3. This part tends to be difficult for parents, but it's important. The more the parents can get specific about what they would actually say to their child, the greater the likelihood that the parents will be able to carry this out at home.

Homework 6.1: Practice Conversational Skills. "Try out one of the suggestions to practice conversational skills that you wrote on the worksheet."

Notes for Group Format
It can be useful to poll parents about the conversational skills problems they see, and the problems they intend to prioritize targeting, so that

the clinician gets a quick sense of the needs of the group without taking too much time. When parents are completing the worksheet, the clinician can walk around and highlight positive examples of antecedents for the group.

3 Handling Boredom and Conflict during the Playdate when Best Efforts Fail

Section goal: If the antecedents, despite your best efforts, aren't working, there are some strategies to deal with behavior problems as they are happening. Watch out for: Parents who don't understand the delicate balance of being subtle yet still intervening.

"In the past two sessions, we have discussed antecedents to prevent boredom and conflict on playdates, such as having your child and the friend plan out what to do and discussing with your child how to be a good host. We learned these things in line with Steps 2 and 3 on the PFC Pyramid (Handout 1.1)."

"Antecedents should be the first thing to try, but sometimes antecedents don't work perfectly. If your child has trouble being a good host, then one conversation isn't going to change things all at once. So, what do you do when, despite your best efforts at setting up good antecedents, it is the middle of the playdate and the children are having boredom or conflict?"

"First, you as the parent have to be very clever during the playdate. Basically, you have to monitor the playdate so that you can catch early signs of boredom or conflict happening, but you have to look as though you are not monitoring the playdate or else it will appear strange to the peer. You will see parents of toddlers having playdates where both parents are standing next to their children to monitor their behavior. Your child may need this level of monitoring, but because of your child's age, it will look weird if you do this. Therefore, you have to monitor while appearing to not be monitoring. How could you do this?"

Solicit ideas from parents, because this is a good way to keep them engaged. Also, they know best what is feasible for their family. Some things that have worked for parents in the past:

- Sit in the next room where the kids can't see you and pretend to be reading or working while you are listening to what is going on.
- Walk around the house cleaning or putting things away so that you pass by the room where your child is or have to go into that room to put something away every so often.
- If your child is playing in the backyard with the peer, do some gardening outside or wash dishes/cook in the kitchen if you can look out the kitchen window into the yard. Keep the window or back door open so you can hear.
- With younger children (ages 6–8), it is more normal to look as if you are monitoring more than with older children (ages 9–11).

"This probably sounds very intensive for you, and it is, but the idea is that doing this is most important during the first playdates. You do not have to do this forever. You can ease off once your child develops better friendship skills and hits it off with some peers."

"How have you been able to tell in the past that boredom is starting to happen in the middle of the playdate?" Some markers you might see in the peer or your child:

- Starting to look uninterested in the game, or unenthusiastic
- One child wandering around the room doing something else while the other child continues playing
- Voicing that they want to do something else
- Asking what they want to do next but both come up with "I don't know" as an answer

"Ideally, your child will be skilled enough to pick up on these signs and ask the peer if they want to do something else, but if boredom is happening in the middle of the playdate and your child is not picking up on it, there are some things that a parent can do to intervene:

- Call both children into the kitchen for snacks. You can also have both children help you prepare the snacks as a fun new activity for them, if the preparation is not that complicated.
- If it looks like the peer is getting bored and your child doesn't notice it, pull your child aside and tell them to find out if the peer wants to do something else.
- If your child and the peer are not playing together, pull your child aside and suggest ways to get the peer involved again.
- If the children can't come up with things to do, you may have to suggest some ideas. This is why it is good to have back-up activities.

The clinician can ask parents which of these suggestions they think might work for their family.

"What about if the children start having conflict in the middle of a playdate? Again, ideally, your child will be skilled enough to problem solve and resolve this conflict with the peer, but if conflict is happening and your child is not handling this effectively, there are some things that parents can do to intervene."

Handout 6.3: *Instructing Your Child during a Playdate*

The main idea of Handout 6.3 is that if parents see conflict happening, they basically have four choices:

- Don't do anything and just talk to your child about it later after the peer leaves.

- Do one of the distraction strategies because maybe that will diffuse the situation, and don't say anything to your child about it until after the peer leaves.
- Whisper or say something quickly to your child in the moment to correct the behavior.
- Pull your child aside for a moment and talk to your child to correct the behavior.

"There are pros and cons of all these choices. Guidelines for how you can decide which choice to make are listed in the handout. The main benefit of using strategies #1 and #2 is that it might help to keep the playdate tone positive and your child not embarrassed. However, if your child's behavior is really bad, then you should intervene more directly because the guest will have already noticed. A benefit of using strategies #3 and #4 is that children learn best when they are instructed in the moment, and they have the opportunity to practice better behavior right there and then. If you wait until later, you will still have a chance to help your child, but your child may not know as well what you're talking about. However, if talking to your child is going to cause a fight, it may be better to do this after the peer leaves."

Ask parents what strategy they think would work best for their child, and why. Consider the child's age, type of behavior problem, and the extent to which the child is easily embarrassed. Encouraging parents to apply what they are learning to their own child will keep them engaged and also raise the probability that they will carry out the skills at home.

Explain the "secret signal" reference in the handout: "If your child is embarrassed easily, consider using a secret signal to let your child know that you want them to change their behavior or that you need to speak to them. To do this, speak to your child in advance about letting you be like their sports coach; just like the coach sends secret signals to players in the game to let the players know what to do without the other team knowing, you can send a secret signal to your child to help your child with making friends. Frame the discussion so that the child feels you are on their side and that you understand how hard it can be to remember the rules of being a good host. So, for example, you could arrange with your child that you will pull your ear to remind your child that they should ask the guest if the guest is having fun or if the guest would like to play something else."

"Look under the "do's" and "don'ts" on the final page of the handout. Note the ways in which the parent in example #4 is following these guidelines. What do you notice?" Some ideas:

- The parent praises the child for agreeing to turn behavior around.
- Even though the child is grumpy about it, the parent doesn't get pulled into the grumpiness.
- The parent is specific about what behavior they want to see.

- The parent is encouraging.
- The parent stays calm.

Role-Play 6.1: Handling Problem Behavior 1. Ideally, this role-play has a "parent," "child," and "guest." However, the clinician can take the child role (with an imaginary guest), and the parent can play the parent role. Child and guest are playing. Guest gets bored and starts playing something else; child doesn't notice and keeps playing the same thing. The parent should coach the child to handle this situation better. It is up to the parent to choose which method (of #1 to #4) they want to practice. If the parent chooses #1 or #2, role-play the discussion with the child after the guest leaves.

Role-Play 6.2: Handling Problem Behavior 2 (if time). "Parent," "child," and "guest" again. Child misbehaves and parent instructs the child. The parent should choose a different strategy to try out than in the previous role-play, but one that the parent finds relevant for their child.

Clinicians should remember the guidelines for debriefing after role-plays (and video recording reviews) to make this a positive and useful experience for the parent.

Skip if not an issue: Parents may bring up the idea that "what if I talk to my child (scenario #4) and then my child breaks the rule again right away as soon as they get back to the peer?"

- If your child breaks the rule again right away, warn them with "If you don't share, you'll have to take a break from playing for a little bit." If your child starts following the rules again, praise!
- If your child breaks the rule a second time after the warning, follow through on your consequence and give your child a time out. Tell the peer that your child will be right back. Have your child go to another room for a brief amount of time, such as 5 minutes for a child ages 6–8 and probably no more than 10 minutes for a child ages 9–11, unless your child is really angry and needs more time to calm down. So long as your child has calmed down, remind them of the rules and let them go back and play.
- The one warning then the time out is the generally suggested way to handle mild infractions of rules. However, if your child has done a serious rule violation (e.g., pushed the peer), you can send your child directly to time out without a warning.

Skip if not an issue: Some parents may have concerns about giving their child a time out while the guest is there or may have questions about how to give a time out.

- It is still appropriate for an older child (ages 9–11) to have a time out, but it might be better to not call it a time out. You can just say to your child, "if you keep arguing about who is winning, then you will have to stop playing for a while." Then instead of a specified "time out," you just take your child aside for a break, and tell your child that they have to apologize to the guest when they are ready to come back.

- Is a time out embarrassing for your child? Yes, a bit, but if your child is behaving very badly, it is probably your best option. If you let the bad behavior go, the guest will decide that they don't like your child and won't want to come back to play because you don't do anything about it. A time out also ends the argument between the children. To minimize embarrassment, stay calm and don't lose your temper when you are giving the time out. Act like the time out is not a big deal, even though you remain firm in carrying it out.

Skip if not an issue: "What if the guest is being rude? Explain to your child that they still follow the rules of being a good host, and they never have to invite that guest over again. This is another good reason to have short playdates at first until you know this guest can behave. Generally speaking, unless the guest is doing something dangerous or physically hurting your child, your child should try to be polite; this is hard for some children who perceive this as unfair. If the guest's behavior is very out of control, then you as the parent are free to contact the guest's parent. Although you have less control over the guest's behavior than you do over your child's behavior, you can still praise your child for handling bad guest behavior, and you can instruct both children together about the rules of your house."

Skip if not an issue: "What if both children are in an argument and it is partly your child's fault and also partly the fault of the guest (in your opinion)? You can give both children a break where they both do something else for a little while to cool down, and then come back to playing (in essence, separate time outs). Especially if the children are young, have both children apologize to each other and move on to a different activity. Later, use active listening with your child and be sure to support your child's feeling of being wronged. If your child feels like you only criticize and never take their side, your child will be less likely to listen to your suggestions for how to improve things in the future. You can also instruct your child using corrective feedback about what your child can do next time."

Playdate Progress: "I am continuing to encourage you to work on setting up playdates for your child. Again, every family needs to go at their own pace and is in a different situation, so I understand and want to support your individual goals. The skills we have learned so far are:"

- With your child, discuss who you would like to invite for a playdate.
- Help your child talk to the friend to decide what to play.
- Prepare fun activities for the playdate.
- Ensure your child is not tired or hungry before the playdate.
- Before the playdate, talk to your child about being a good host.
- Put away any toys that are likely to cause conflict.

- (New Skill) Intervene in the playdate to stop early signs of boredom.
- (New Skill) Intervene in the playdate to stop early signs of conflict.

"Remember that it's better if you can try to manipulate the antecedents first to make the playdate go smoothly. However, if that doesn't work, try the other strategies during the playdate to stop early signs of boredom or conflict."

Homework 6.2: Continue Relationship-Building. "Continue Special Time, active listening, praise/corrective feedback, etc."

Notes for Group Format

Clinicians might want to take a poll before the role-plays about which strategies parents expect their child might respond to best. This will help clinicians direct the role-plays to illustrate those strategies, based on the needs of the group.

4 Video Recording Review (Optional)

Section goal: Illustrating skills that have been covered so far in a relevant way. Watch out for: Parents may feel uncomfortable or worried about negative evaluation.

"We will be going over another video recording of yours to demonstrate the skills we have been learning so far."

Again, the clinician should think about which video clip to choose based on what would be useful for the parent at this point in terms of the skills focused on, or the type of feedback the clinician could give based on the video. Given that the sessions are now touching on how to intervene in a playdate, this could be a good time to show a video of the child and friend interacting (if that type of video is available). Discuss the video with the parent.

Notes for Group Format

If running PFC in group format, think about whose video to choose. We recommend that clinicians ask permission from the parent and give the parent a heads-up in advance. When discussing the video, clinicians should continue to prime the group to give specific positive feedback to the parent and to model this.

5 Ending Business

Pass out the Homework List and Parent Satisfaction form (optional).

The Homework List is for parents to take home with them. Parents fill out the Parent Satisfaction form and give it to the clinician before leaving.

Notes for Group Format

The Parent Satisfaction form may be more useful if PFC is being delivered in group format.

Session 7   Teaching Your Child Social Skills, Part 2

1 Review of Homework

Section goal: To get parents excited about playdates and inspired to have more. Watch out for: Parents feeling stuck or behind; parents having difficulty balancing quantity versus quality of playdates.

Review the homework about working on conversational skills while supporting parents and troubleshooting when needed.

Review the big picture steps about setting up a high-quality, successful playdate:

1   Choosing the right potential friend
2   Helping your child to invite the friend for a playdate
3   Preparing for the playdate to prevent boredom and conflict
4   Teaching your child good friendship skills
5   Intervening in the playdate if boredom and conflict are starting to occur

If the clinician wrote down the list of steps on a flip chart or board the previous session, it is usually effective to pull out the chart and add the sixth step.

"This week we will be working on how to teach your child more friendship skills, and also, the last step in this process, which is:"

6   Debriefing with your child after the playdate

More parents will have had playdates by this session, and they are usually excited to share. Review where parents are at in playdate progress.

Some parents may be unsure whether to focus on quantity versus quality of playdates. In general, we recommend focusing on quality; it is better for the parent to arrange 1–2 high-quality playdates by the end of the PFC program than to try to arrange as many playdates as possible. However, quantity is also useful (within reason). The child may get benefits from learning to play with a variety of different children (such as exposure

DOI: 10.4324/9781003221715-9

to different play styles), more playdates may also help the child to be less lonely, and the child may be more likely to find a peer to befriend if they have more playdate opportunities.

Notes for Group Format
Sometimes at this point, there are large differences between parents in how well they have carried out the playdate (or whether they have carried it out), and these can be difficult for the clinician to handle. Parents sometimes feel guilty about these differences. It can be useful for the clinician to remind everyone that every parent is in a different situation (and has a different child), so it is expected that every parent will be setting up playdates at their own pace.

2 Helping Your Child Learn Good Friendship Skills, Part 3

Section goal: To give parents tools for teaching their child emotion regulation. Watch out for: Some parents may have trouble teaching this to their children because they find it difficult to regulate their own emotions themselves.

Remind parents: "This is another social skill that parents can teach their children (like game-playing skills and conversational skills), which is part of Step 2 in the PFC Pyramid (Handout 1.1)."

"Everyone gets upset, angry, or sad sometimes, and this is natural. But, many children with ADHD have trouble handling their negative emotions when they happen. When the smallest thing goes wrong, your child might get very upset very quickly. It might seem like your child goes from 0 to 100 in a few seconds and can't seem to let the anger go. Or, maybe your child gets disappointed and gets hurt feelings easily, and then will be upset for a long time or cry more easily than other children the same age, sometimes in front of peers. These are all problems with dealing with negative emotions." The clinician can ask parents whether they see these issues in their child, and how it affects their child's peer relationships. This will help parents personalize the material to their own situation and engage them in the content.

The clinician can illustrate these concepts using the hand brain demonstration: "We are learning more and more about how the brain works, and what we are learning will help you understand what your child is experiencing. Your brain is shaped like your hand. Here is the spinal cord and brainstem in the neck (wrist), and here in the center of the brain by the stem is the area that generates your emotional reactions, called the limbic system (thumb lying in palm). The outer part of your brain forms a layer around the emotional center (fold other four fingers over). This outer part is called the prefrontal cortex, and it is in charge of your rational thinking, logic, and reason. (Show parents how the orientation of the hand model matches up to the orientation of your head.) When we get emotional (wiggle thumb), if the emotion is too strong, we flip our lid (flip up four fingers), and this can make us lose reason and rational thinking. Then, we can do things we regret or say things we don't mean. A child has to practice being aware of the emotions bubbling up early (wiggle thumb) so that they can learn to recognize and deal with them before the emotions get too strong and they flip their lids."

The clinician may find it useful to watch a video that shows the hand brain demonstration or to show such a video to parents. (Search "Daniel Siegal Hand Model" or "Flipping Your Lid.")

Handout 7.1: *Dealing with Negative Emotions*

"Handout 7.1 provides tips to help your child handle anger and sadness. The first step is helping your child to recognize and label their emotions. This is a great exercise for children who seem to be fine one minute and emotional the next minute in a way that is hard for parents to predict. Strategies for dealing with negative emotions won't work unless your child first realizes that they are having the emotion in the first place. Ideally, your child becomes able to recognize that the emotion is starting early on so that they can work on managing it before it gets too strong." The clinician can ask parents if they think this step would help their child.

"The second step is helping your child to come up with plans for self-regulation and calming down. It might be helpful to practice these things with your child in role-plays. Or, if your child tends to get upset when playing games (for instance, when losing), practice playing games with your child while you talk to your child about working on this skill. This practice will help your child get better at dealing with negative emotions when in peer situations."

"Some children like the hand brain demonstration, especially older children. If you think it would help your child understand better, show the hand brain demonstration to your child as part of this discussion."

Consider asking parents to reflect on this idea: "Having negative emotions is part of being human, so we can't expect them to go away entirely. In fact, trying to make them go away entirely sometimes makes things worse. Negative emotions are also important to experience in some situations and can make our lives richer. The goal is for children to get better at realizing when they are happening and to use strategies to help calm down, so they do not feel over-run by their emotions and so strong emotions do not get in the way of their peer relationships." The movie *Inside Out* provides a good depiction of negative and positive emotions working together.

To encourage homework completion, the clinician might ask parents to specify what from the handout they would like to try with their child, when they plan to do it, and any questions or barriers they can foresee.

Homework 7.1: Practice Dealing with Negative Emotions. "Have this discussion or practice with your child about dealing with negative emotions."

Notes for Group Format
Parents could mark the strategies in Handout 7.1 that they already do, that they would like to try, and any that they have questions about. The clinician could circle around the room and get a sense of answers, and then report back to the group about patterns they observe.

3 Giving Effective Feedback after the Playdate

Section goal: There is a good opportunity after a playdate to debrief with the child and reinforce positive social behaviors and to lay the groundwork for better behaviors next time. Watch out for: Because children will be on the defensive, parents need to remember to incorporate warmth and positivity into this conversation.

The clinician can reference the steps that are written on the flip chart or whiteboard and brought out during homework review. "Let's turn back to these steps for setting up a high-quality playdate. We have a new one to talk about today, which is how to debrief with your child after the playdate is done. This is also part of Step 2 on the PFC Pyramid (Handout 1.1)."

"Once the playdate is over, this is a great opportunity to give your child some feedback about their behavior with the friend. However, consider what we have been learning up to now about how to give effective praise and corrective feedback to your child, and how to help your child to be more receptive to your guidance. What do you think are good principles to remember when you are debriefing with your child after the playdate?" The clinician can solicit responses (this will help keep parents more engaged) and then give out Handout 7.2. Alternatively, the clinician can give the handout and ask parents to identify the tips that would be useful for their family.

Handout 7.2: *Debriefing after a Playdate*

This handout provides tips for giving effective feedback after the playdate. It can be useful to remind parents that children may be defensive during this conversation, especially if they know they did not behave perfectly during the playdate. "Have you ever had a time when a boss, teacher, or parent approached you to talk about how you performed, and you felt tense, anticipating the worst?" Ask parents how the other person could have allayed their anxiety. Ask parents to consider what could help allay their child's anxiety about debriefing.

If parents think the suggestions they are providing in the debriefing will be too hard for their child to remember or to carry out the next time, consider developing a reward plan to make an extra incentive. Right before the next playdate, parents can tell the child that "next time if you do (positive social behavior), afterward you will get (reward)." Then, after the playdate, the parent can debrief with the child about how well the child carried out the skill they had talked about in advance and give the child whatever reward that was earned.

Role-Play 7.1: Debriefing. First, ask the parent to identify a strategy they wish to use in the debrief. By this point in PFC, the clinician may already have a good sense of the behaviors the child tends to show on playdates and also the parent's concerns. In this role-play, the clinician can play the "child," either with the parent pretending to be a peer, or with an imaginary peer. In the child role, the clinician can act out some negative and some positive behaviors that the child is likely to show. Then, the parent adopts the "parent" role and practices debriefing with the child (using the strategy decided upon).

Playdate Progress:

"For this week, work on hosting a playdate for your child. The skills we have learned so far are:"

- With your child, discuss who you would like to invite for a playdate.
- Help your child talk to the friend to decide what to play.
- Prepare fun activities for the playdate.
- Ensure your child is not tired or hungry before the playdate.
- Before the playdate, talk to your child about being a good host.
- Put away any toys that are likely to cause conflict.
- Intervene in the playdate to stop early signs of boredom.
- Intervene in the playdate to stop early signs of conflict.
- (New Skill) Debrief with your child after the playdate.

"Debriefing with your child after the playdate can also be used as an antecedent for helping the next playdate to go better."

Homework 7.2: Continue Relationship-Building. "Continue Special Time, active listening, praise/corrective feedback, etc."

Notes for Group Format
In this role-play, there could be two parents who act out the roles of the two children and then two more parents who act out the roles of the parents of the two children. Each "parent" debriefs with their "child."

4 Video Recording Review (Optional)

Section goal: Illustrating skills that have been covered so far in a relevant way. Watch out for: Parents may feel uncomfortable or worried about negative evaluation.

"We will be going over another video recording of you with your child to demonstrate various aspects of parental friendship coaching."

Again, the clinician should think about which video clip to choose based on what would be useful for the parent at this point in terms of the skills focused on, or the type of feedback the clinician could give based on the video. Discuss the video with the parent. Solicit the parent's impressions from watching the video, as well as (potentially) any places where the parent felt they were unsure about what to do.

Notes for Group Format

If running PFC in group format, think about whose video to choose. We recommend that clinicians ask permission from the parent and give the parent a heads-up in advance. When discussing the video, clinicians should continue to prime the group to give specific positive feedback to the parent and to model this.

5 Ending Business

Pass out the Homework List and Parent Satisfaction form (optional).

The Homework List is for parents to take home with them. Parents fill out the Parent Satisfaction form and give it to the clinician before leaving.

Notes for Group Format

The Parent Satisfaction form may be more useful if PFC is being delivered in group format.

Session 8   Preparing for a Playdate as a Guest

1 Review of Homework

Section goal: To get parents excited about playdates and inspired to have more. Watch out for: Parents who feel stuck and have not had a playdate yet, or parents who had a playdate but it did not go well.

Review the homework about handling negative emotions, and troubleshoot with parents about any difficulties. It can be useful to remind parents that like any skill, this one will take practice and repetition. In fact, it would be astounding if the child showed improvement right away.

Review the big picture steps about setting up a high-quality, successful playdate:

1   Choosing the right potential friend
2   Helping your child to invite the friend for a playdate
3   Preparing for the playdate to prevent boredom and conflict
4   Teaching your child good friendship skills
5   Intervening in the playdate if boredom and conflict are starting to occur
6   Debriefing with your child after the playdate

The clinician can reference the flip chart or whiteboard if the steps were written there previously.

"This week we will be working on the step that comes after a successful playdate":

7   Preparing your child for a playdate as a guest

More parents will have had playdates by this session, and they are usually excited to share. Review and troubleshoot as needed.

Notes for Group Format

The challenges we usually face concern parents being in very different stages of the playdate process and needing different types of support.

DOI: 10.4324/9781003221715-10

2 Preparing for a Playdate as a Guest

Section goal: The parent has less ability to structure, monitor, control, and intervene in the playdate at another family's house relative to when hosting. The parent should try to still do this without it being weird or impractical. Watch out for: Parents feeling overwhelmed or too busy to spend the time needed to set up the antecedents to make a guest playdate go well. Parents who don't know if they can trust the other family, or trust their own child, enough to have a guest playdate.

"Suppose your child's playdate is successful and the other family wants to reciprocate? In that case, the other child's parents will probably invite your child over as a guest. This is a great (and important) step to celebrate. It means that the peer had a good time on the playdate you hosted and is telling their parents that they want to have another playdate with your child. It also means that the parents of the peer have a favorable impression of your child and your family. These are all very positive outcomes, especially if your child has not done well on playdates in the past."

Check in with parents about whether the idea of sending their child on a playdate as a guest makes them nervous, and why that is. This will help keep parents engaged and also help the clinician understand the family's particular situation.

"Sending your child on a playdate as a guest is a big step, however, because you have less control over what happens and less ability to monitor your child to make sure your child is behaving. If your child is not ready, then you might want to keep doing host playdates and minimize guest playdates until your child has better friendship skills. This will be easier if you have host playdates with several different peers instead of the same peer all the time, because if you keep having good playdates with the same peer, that peer's family is more likely to start inviting your child over as a guest and then you will be in the awkward position of having to come up with an excuse for why you can't go."

"Sooner or later, however, you need to let your child be a guest, because this is important for your child's friendship development. Fortunately, there are still some antecedents you can use to increase the probability that things will go well on a playdate as a guest. These are part of Steps 2 and 3 on the PFC Pyramid (Handout 1.1)."

"First, you can prepare your child by going over the rules of being a good guest, similar to the way you went over the rules of being a good host. You want to discuss these rules with your child, praise your child for the ones that they do well, and pick one main rule to target for improvement."

Handout 8.1: *Being a Good Guest*

The main points of Handout 8.1 are the headings in bold.

- Perhaps do role-plays with your child to practice a specific skill with which your child has trouble.
- Consider drawing up a contract where your child will get a reward after the playdate if they display the specific skill you are working on, but make sure you have a realistic plan to find out if your child showed the skill or not. Praise may be enough of a reward for some children (especially young children). With other children, earning TV or screen time, or privileges such as a choice of a movie to watch or going for ice cream, are effective rewards.
- Be very specific about the behavior that you want your child to do. "Play nice with the friend" is too vague. It helps to spell things out explicitly. (Remember the principles of effective praise and corrective feedback.)
- Remind your child of the expected behavior again right before you drop them off for the playdate (or right before the other family comes to pick your child up).

The clinician might ask parents which strategies on Handout 8.1 are feasible and useful for their family.

Role-Play 8.1: Being a Good Guest. "Parent" (played by parent) and "child" (played by clinician) discuss how to be a good guest. It can be useful for the clinician to ask the parent how they think their child will respond, and if the parent has any concerns about how this conversation will go. The clinician should try to act out the behaviors that the parent's child would show so that the parent can practice handling these concerns. Discuss the role-play afterward, remembering the suggested 4:1 ratio of praise-to-corrective feedback.

"A second antecedent to prevent behavior problems when your child is a guest is to keep the first 'guest' playdate short and structured. If that goes well, then you can be more casual about future playdates. You may need to talk to the other parent about this. This can be hard to do in a sneaky way that accomplishes what you need but doesn't reveal that you are concerned about your child behaving badly."

"Sometimes parents at this point are thinking about whether they should tell the other parent that their child has ADHD. Every family needs to make this decision for themselves, and there isn't one rule that works for everyone. We will be talking more about this topic in the next session too. What are your thoughts about whether to tell?" Help parents work through their thoughts on this issue. Some considerations:

- It could be a bad idea initially unless you already know and trust this other parent. It can set up negative expectations about your child and stigma.
- However, telling another parent could allow them to be more structured and understanding with your child, particularly if you know and trust the parent.

Handout 8.2: *Encouraging a Structured Playdate as a Guest*

Handout 8.2 contains some examples of how a parent could handle it if they have concerns about their child's behavior but do not want to fully communicate this to the other parent at this time. Ask parents to read the example scripts (reprinted below) and discuss how this might apply or not apply to their family. Note that in both scripts, Parent 2 makes sure to emphasize how their child likes the peer and will have fun on the playdate.

Example 1

(Parent 2 is concerned that Carly will not behave well in a long, unstructured playdate but does not want to communicate this to Parent 1 at this time).

Parent 1: We'd like to have Carly come over on Saturday.
Parent 2: Carly will be so excited, thanks so much! What did you have in mind?
Parent 1: Oh hmmm, I don't know, maybe she could come over in the morning and hang out until we have our family barbeque that afternoon. And there's a pool out there too.
Parent 2: That sounds fun. We have a bunch of stuff to do on Saturday morning; any chance that I could drop her off for the barbeque? What time would that start?
Parent 1: Sure, we'll probably fire up the grill around 2 and then cook around 3. Maybe the girls can go swimming before the cookout?
Parent 2: That sounds perfect. I'll drop Carly off with her bathing suit at 2 and then check in around 4 to see if she is all done eating. It is so kind of you to invite her and she will really have fun.

Example 2

(Parent 2 is concerned that D'Shawn will not behave well when playing competitive video games and wants to let Parent 1 know this without seeming overly concerned or controlling).

Parent 1: Tyler says that he and D'Shawn want to play this weekend. I thought I would take them to Playland arcade.
Parent 2: Oh, D'Shawn will like that. I also know he likes Tyler and has said a lot of good things about him.
Parent 1: Great! How is Saturday afternoon?
Parent 2: That will be good. D'Shawn will be over the moon with excitement. By the way, sometimes he can get overstimulated with video games, especially when they're competitive, so if you're seeing that feel free to make them off limits for a time so he can cool down.

Parent 1: Actually, Tyler gets that way too; I'll just make them off limits for both the boys.

Parent 2: Awesome. Should I drop him off at your house or just meet at Playland?

Some parents may ask what to do if Tyler's parent dismisses the comment about D'Shawn getting overstimulated. In this situation, D'Shawn's parent has a choice to make. They can let it go and hope for the best (while also talking to D'Shawn in advance about good behavior in an arcade, as an antecedent before the playdate). Or, they can be more explicit with Tyler's parent.

Notes for Group Format

To check in with more families, it can be useful to ask parents to mark, on Handout 8.1, which strategies they definitely want to try, which ones they are not sure about trying just yet, and any ones for which they have questions.

Clinicians can also poll parents to ask about their feelings or questions about having a guest playdate. Sometimes if parents have anxieties about the process, we have found that it can be more useful to hear reassurance from other parents than from the clinician.

3 Picking Up Your Child from a Playdate as a Guest

Section goal: Parents need to make efforts if they want any real feedback about their child's behavior as a guest. Watch out for: Some parents find it anxiety provoking to having this conversation, or they may find it difficult to accept negative feedback about their child.

"When you pick your child up from a playdate as a guest (or the other family drops your child off), this is a good time to touch base with the other parent so that you know how your child did. This is important for two reasons. First, if your child had a behavior problem, this way you will know about it and be able to work with your child on correcting it, which helps you with Step 2 on the PFC Pyramid (Handout 1.1)."

"Second, it will allow the other parent to get to know you. If your child had a behavior problem, the other parent will be more likely to invite your child over again if the other parent thinks that you care about your child's behavior and that you are working on the behavior with your child. This falls under Step 3 on the PFC Pyramid (Handout 1.1)."

Handout 8.3: *Picking Up Your Child from a Playdate as a Guest*

The main points of Handout 8.3 are in bold. Ask parents to remember a scenario when they invited over a child who behaved badly. Ask: "What would that other child's parent have to say to you in order for you to tell them the truth?" Getting parents to generate ideas will help them to stay involved and also will allow the clinician to learn the norms in the parents' neighborhood or culture, which can differ between parents. Bottom line though, parents usually conclude that just saying, "was everything ok?" may not be enough to get a truthful answer.

"Here are some phrases that other parents have said were helpful:"

- How did the girls get along?
- How did Carly behave today?
- Did any concerns about Carly's behavior come up today that I should know about?
- At home we have been working on sharing. Can you let me know how she did with sharing today so I can talk to her about it?

"The important thing to remember is that if your child showed behavior problems, you want to show you are on top of your child's behavior, but without seeming overly concerned or anxious. You want to give the other parent a good impression that you care about your child's behavior and are working on it, but you don't want to seem like your child's behavior is so bad you can't control it. You want to keep a positive tone, while taking what the other parent says seriously."

The clinician can acknowledge that this is a tough balance, and ask parents how they think they might accomplish this. The clinician can also ask parents what aspects of this process feel easier versus more challenging to them.

Ask parents, "what do you think is a good way to respond if the host parent tells you some concerns about your child's behavior?" Some ideas:

- Try to not be defensive, not criticize the host parent for how they handled things, and not lose your temper.
- Show that you take the feedback seriously. Show that you are listening.
- If your child objectively did something bad, apologize calmly and sincerely but without seeming overly upset or anxious about it.

"If you don't agree with what the host parent said, stay calm and don't burn any bridges. Go home later and think about what was true and what you can teach your child from this experience. If eventually you decide that what the host parent said was garbage, you can just forget it and you don't have to see that family again."

"If the host parent tells you things were great and that your child was well behaved, be sure to praise your child for it, and put a mental note to invite that family for the next playdate soon."

Role-Play 8.2: Picking Up Your Child. Parent and clinician role-play being two parents checking in after a playdate about the child's behavior. Remember the principles to help role-plays be a positive and effective learning experience for parents. Based on what is useful for the parent, consider role-playing a situation where some behavior problems came up.

Playdate Progress:

"For this week, work on hosting a playdate for your child. The skills we have learned so far are:"

- With your child, discuss who you would like to invite for a playdate.
- Help your child talk to the friend to decide what to play.
- Prepare fun activities for the playdate.
- Ensure your child is not tired or hungry before the playdate.
- Before the playdate, talk to your child about being a good host.
- Put away any toys that are likely to cause conflict.
- Intervene in the playdate to stop early signs of boredom.
- Intervene in the playdate to stop early signs of conflict.
- Debrief with your child after the playdate.

Also, it is useful to think about how to prepare for being a guest. We learned some new skills related to that this week:

- (New Skill) Prepare your child to be a good guest.
- (New Skill) Check in with the parent of the peer about your child's behavior.

"As in other sessions, please keep working on playdates for your child."

Homework 8.1: Continue Relationship-Building. "Continue Special Time, active listening, praise/corrective feedback, etc."

Notes for Group Format

This is another place where the group can be helpful in brainstorming with one another about how to handle any negative feedback from another parent. Sometimes parents prefer to hear this information from other families who have lived experience with ADHD and who may understand their situation in their neighborhood better than the clinician.

4 Video Recording Review (Optional)

Section goal: Illustrating skills that have been covered so far in a relevant way. Watch out for: Parents may feel uncomfortable or worried about negative evaluation.

"We will be going over another video recording of you with your child to demonstrate various aspects of parental friendship coaching."

Again, the clinician should think about which video clip to choose based on what would be useful for the parent at this point in terms of the skills focused on, or the type of feedback the clinician could give based on the video. Discuss the video with the parent and solicit parent impressions and suggestions.

Notes for Group Format

If running PFC in group format, think about whose video to choose. We recommend that clinicians ask permission from the parent and give the parent a heads-up in advance. When discussing the video, clinicians should continue to prime the group to give specific positive feedback to the parent and to model this.

5 Ending Business

Pass out the Homework List and Parent Satisfaction form (optional).
The Homework List is for parents to take home with them. Parents fill out the Parent Satisfaction form and give it to the clinician before leaving.

Notes for Group Format

The Parent Satisfaction form may be more useful if PFC is being delivered in group format.

Session 9   Meeting New Peers

1 Review of Homework

Section goal: To get parents excited about playdates and inspired to have more. Watch out for: Parents who feel stuck and have not had a playdate yet, or parents who had a playdate but it did not go well.

Today's homework review focuses on troubleshooting potential issues in playdates.

Review the big picture steps about setting up a high-quality, successful playdate:

1   Choosing the right potential friend
2   Helping your child to invite the friend for a playdate
3   Preparing for the playdate to prevent boredom and conflict
4   Teaching your child good friendship skills
5   Intervening in the playdate if boredom and conflict are starting to occur
6   Debriefing with your child after the playdate
7   Preparing your child for a playdate as a guest

The clinician can reference the flip chart or whiteboard where these steps are written.

More parents will have had playdates by this session, and they are usually excited to share. Review and troubleshoot as needed.

"Hopefully you are feeling off to a good start in terms of having better playdates and deepening friendships. However, today, we will also be talking about ways to broaden your child's social circle so that they have more friendship opportunities in the future. These skills fall under Part 3 of the PFC Pyramid (Handout 1.1)."

Notes for Group Format

There are two sessions left, including today, and it may be useful to ask each parent in the group to identify a friendship-related homework goal that they want to carry out before the end of the PFC program.

DOI: 10.4324/9781003221715-11

2 Meeting New Friends

Section goal: To build parents' empathy for why it's hard to meet new kids and to identify the skills that are needed to make new friends. Watch out for: This section is not needed for all parents. Some parents have kids who do this just fine; the problem is in deepening friendships. If this is not a needed skill, skip or skim.

"Some parents have a hard time identifying a peer to contact for a playdate, so they quickly run out of options for potential friends for their child. If this is your situation, then it could help your child to meet some new friends that are outside of the existing social circle of peers that they already know." Check in with parents about how much this situation applies to them.

"Some kids already have one really good friend. This is terrific and something to celebrate! However, there are some reasons why ideally your child should have more than one good friend. Can you think of why that might be?" Some ideas:

- In case the one friend is busy or moves away or becomes interested in other things (or friends), it's good for your child to have other options.
- It's good for children, in the long term, to learn how to get along with a diverse range of peers with different personality styles. Your child will learn slightly different things from each friend.

"Skills regarding meeting new friends are especially needed for families in three situations:"

- Your child doesn't approach new kids appropriately. They may either be too shy, or may barge in, or may get hurt when other children don't accept them.
- Your child has a problem with being drawn to the kids who are bad influences, who won't like them, or who are not true friends. They may be drawn to the younger kid who your child can boss around.
- Your child has a bad reputation at school. These skills might help your child change their reputation or meet new friends who don't already know their reputation.

Check in with families about whether they think their child could benefit from meeting some new peers, and why. This information will help the clinician tailor the skills in this section.

Ask parents: "Imagine you're at a party and you don't really know anybody. There are many small groups of adults talking to each other."

- What are some of the difficulties of this situation?
- How might you feel emotionally during this experience?

- How can you best break into the social circle?
- What are some of the rules for joining a new group?

Discuss and elicit some ideas from parents. "This exercise is done for two reasons—first, to build empathy for how difficult meeting new friends can be for children, and second, to help parents come up with some of the rules that will help their children. Many of the same rules apply for kids as for adults in terms of joining a group, except that kids don't necessarily introduce themselves formally. Instead, kids usually just ask to join an existing activity."

Handout 9.1: *How Children Join Others at Play*

Show parents Handout 9.1 and ask, "What are the problems you see in your child? What are the issues that you see you child having with these steps?" This question helps parents connect the skills to their child's unique situation and helps the clinician and parents know what to work on.

The following are the main points to take away from the handout:

- Kids should be alert for the right time to join in a group. Some kids intrude and don't wait for a good break. Other kids just sit to the side and never join. Timing is important.
- Kids should join in a helpful and nice way.
- Kids should be prepared for rejection and not act upset about it.

Skip if not an issue: "It can be hard for kids with ADHD to figure out when a good time to join is. If this is true for your child you may need to practice that. Your board game time is a good opportunity for teaching this skill. A good time to join in during a quick game (such as Connect Four) is to ask when the game is ending if you can play next game. If it's a longer game or something like a ball or soccer game, wait until there's a pause, a goal, a break, or something like that."

Skip if not an issue: "If your child has trouble dealing with rejection, you should discuss this with your child in advance and role-play with them what they would do if turned down (similar to how we role-play things in here). You can also use the strategies for dealing with negative emotion that we discussed in the last group. Popular children get turned down about 50% of the time they attempt to approach new groups of kids. Popular children don't get upset by it, they just move on to another group of kids, or they play by themselves for a while. They will try again with the same group of kids later and won't hold grudges about having been turned down."

Handout 9.2: *Coaching Your Child to Join Others at Play*

The main points on Handout 9.2 are:

- If your child has trouble joining other children, you can work on this by practicing it with your child at a park where other children are playing, or in a regular peer activity of your child's where you can observe.
- Target whatever the particular problem is that your child has. If it is finding the right time to jump in, you and your child should watch a group of children and discuss when the "right time" would be. If it is never joining, you and your child should role-play what to do and say to join. Then, you can be like a coach from the sidelines and get your child to try out the new skill.
- You have to be clever in this situation, like on playdates. You need to be watching your child but have to pretend you are not watching or else it will look weird to the peers.
- Afterward, remember to praise your child for following the rules of joining. You may have to start praising for 30% correct to keep the ratio of positive: negative closer to 4:1. If your child breaks a rule of joining, use the effective corrective feedback principles.
- No matter what happens, give a lot of praise to your child afterward for trying something new. It is scary to try to meet new peers!

"When preparing your child to meet new peers, try asking your child first (especially older children ages 9–11) what they might do, before you jump in with suggestions. If your child can't come up with anything, try offering your child two alternatives that are both good and letting your child choose." For example:

PARENT: What do you think would be a good thing to do if they don't let you play?
CHILD: I don't know.
PARENT: Which one sounds good to you: Try other kids or try again later?

Role-Play 9.1: Joining New Peers. The parent can play the "parent" role, and the clinician can play the "child" of the parent. The parent should talk to the child about how to join a new group of peers. The role-play should be tailored to whatever problem in joining new peers that the child is experiencing.

"Once your child has hit it off with a peer, you might arrange a playdate:"

PARENT: Is there anyone on the team you would like to invite over to play?
CHILD: I don't know.
PARENT: How about Lucas? You seem to get along with him and you could ask him if he wants to come over.
CHILD: Okay."

"If this is a first playdate with someone from an extracurricular activity, an idea is to take your child and the peer for ice cream (or some other short treat) after the next practice or activity, and then take the peer home." The clinician could ask parents why they think this is a good idea for a first playdate. Some reasons:

- There's a clear thing for the children to do.
- It's easy for the parent to supervise the whole time because it is very brief.
- Most children will like ice cream and therefore find this fun.
- If the child and the peer get along, then there can be a longer playdate the next time.

Notes for Group Format

In our experience, families tend to have children with very different problems related to this topic, even though the overall goal (meeting new peers) is relevant for most families. This can be hard for the clinician in terms of knowing where to focus the group. It may be useful to take a moment to poll parents about which issues they see in their children so that the clinician can get a sense of the group's needs.

3 Parent-to-Parent Networking

Section goal: If parents are friends with other parents who have kids their child's age, this will help their child to make friends too. Watch out for: Some parents have social anxiety or other difficulties, or feel stigma about their child's behavior, which get in the way of them networking.

"You might have noticed from looking at Handout 9.2 that this requires parents to socialize and network with other parents at their child's organized activities and on playgrounds. This is, in fact, what is being asked, and I know that this may not be easy."

"This is yet another way in which the PFC program asks parents of children with ADHD to be 'super parents.' Parents of typically developing children don't need to be well-connected themselves, because their kids naturally make friends without their parents' help. But for children who have friendship problems, there are some reasons why, as a parent, you want to be sociable yourself and meet a lot of other parents." Ask parents why they think this is. Some ideas:

- If other parents know you and like you, they will be more likely to invite your child to things or accept your invitations for playdates.
- If other parents know you and like you, they will be more willing to accept it if your child does not behave perfectly.
- If you know other parents and their children, you will be able to choose who will be a good friendship choice for your child.
- If you know other parents and their children, you will be able to choose whose parents are good at handling your child and accepting your child's behavior if it is not perfect.

Handout 9.3: *Networking with Other Parents*

"This handout lists tips that parents in the PFC program in the past have said were effective for them to make friends with other parents of kids their child's age." Ask parents which ideas they have tried and which they might want to try. The clinician can also ask if parents have ideas that are not on this handout, which could be added to the toolbox to help other parents in the future.

Ask parents what some barriers are to networking with other parents. Parents might bring up:

- Personal histories of peer rejection themselves
- Personal difficulties with their own social anxiety, adult ADHD, depression, or other mental health issues
- Lack of time/too busy
- Stigma about their child's behavior problems (e.g., fear that other people will think they are a bad parent because of their child's behavior, which makes them want to avoid social interactions where they think they might be judged negatively)

If parents do not bring up stigma, the clinician should raise it as something that some parents of children with ADHD have said was an issue. There has also been research finding that this type of stigma prevents parents from arranging social activities for their children and doing friendship coaching behaviors, including in the pilot study of PFC. Ask parents what they have found effective in reducing their feelings of stigma. Here are some ideas that parents have said:

- Meeting other parents of children with ADHD may help some parents realize they are not alone and normalize the experience.
- It may help for parents to remind themselves that experts know that ADHD is not caused by bad parenting, so anyone who thinks that is misinformed and not someone the parent would want to befriend anyway.

"A study showed that parents of children with ADHD often isolated themselves because they thought they were being judged negatively by other parents. Sometimes this was in fact true; however, the extent to which parents of children with ADHD expected that other people were judging them was often greater than the amount that other people were truly judging them." The clinician might ask parents to reflect on this finding and whether they think this applies to them. Clinicians, see:

Norvilitis, J. M., Scime, M. & Lee, J. S. (2002). Courtesy stigma in mothers of children with attention-deficit/hyperactivity disorder: A preliminary investigation. *Journal of Attention Disorders, 6*(2), 61–68. https://doi.org/10.1177%2F108705470200600202

The topic of whether to tell other families that the child has ADHD may have come up in the previous session. It can be useful to follow-up on that topic here or to introduce it for the first time. "Many parents wonder when you tell other parents that your child has ADHD, and when do you not? Ultimately, this is a decision that is best left to each individual family because there's no clear right or wrong answers." Here are some things parents can consider:

- Don't tell immediately. In the meantime, have the peer over for some playdates first so you can get to know the family better. Once your child is invited over to the peer's house as a guest for a playdate, you can think again about whether it is time to tell.
- Tell if it will help the other parent to better understand your child's needs, to be empathetic to your child, and to provide your child with the structures and behavioral supports they need during playdates at the other parent's house.
- Don't tell if the other parent will expect the worst of your child, think you are a bad parent, and not understand. Consider whether you want this type of parent as a friend anyway.

The clinician might ask parents to share their personal guidelines for when they tell versus don't tell others that their child has ADHD, and how these guidelines have been working for their family.

Homework 9.1: Meeting New Peers. "Use one of these strategies to help your child meet new friends/broaden their social circle." The clinician might ask parents to indicate what they plan to try, and when, to encourage homework completion.

Homework 9.2: Continue Relationship-Building. "Continue Special Time, active listening, praise/corrective feedback, etc."

Playdate Progress:

"As in the past sessions, I am encouraging you to keep working on playdates. Here are the skills we have gone over:"

- With your child, discuss who you would like to invite for a playdate.
- Help your child talk to the friend to decide what to play.
- Prepare fun activities for the playdate.
- Ensure your child is not tired or hungry before the playdate.
- Before the playdate, talk to your child about being a good host.
- Put away any toys that are likely to cause conflict.
- Intervene in the playdate to stop early signs of boredom.
- Intervene in the playdate to stop early signs of conflict.
- Debrief with your child after the playdate.
- Prepare your child to be a good guest.
- Check in with the parent of the peer about your child's behavior.

Notes for Group Format
We have found the group format to be especially helpful when discussing parent-to-parent networking and stigma, more than any other topic. Parents appreciate hearing from other parents with lived experience when discussing these topics, often more than they appreciate hearing from clinicians. In this section in particular, we try to encourage parents to advise one another.

4 Video Recording Review (Optional)

Section goal: Illustrating skills that have been covered so far in a relevant way. Watch out for: Parents may feel uncomfortable or worried about negative evaluation.

"We will be going over another video recording of you with your child to demonstrate various aspects of parental friendship coaching."

Again, the clinician should think about which video clip to choose based on what would be useful for the parent at this point in terms of the skills focused on, or the type of feedback the clinician could give based on the video. Discuss the video with the parent, asking for reflections and suggestions.

Notes for Group Format
If running PFC in group format, think about whose video to choose. We recommend that clinicians ask permission from the parent and give the parent a heads-up in advance. When discussing the video, clinicians should continue to prime the group to give specific positive feedback to the parent and to model this.

5 Ending Business

Pass out the Homework List and Parent Satisfaction form (optional).

The Homework List is for parents to take home with them. Parents fill out the Parent Satisfaction form and give it to the clinician before leaving.

Notes for Group Format
The Parent Satisfaction form may be more useful if PFC is being delivered in group format.

Session 10   Getting Ready for the Future

1 Review of Homework

Section goal: To set parents up to continue the momentum in being friendship coaches for their children. Watch out for: Because it is the last session, occasionally, some parents are pulled to misreport the progress made, either by over-reporting or under-reporting.

Check in with parents about the assignment to help children make new friends/broaden their social circle. Ask if parents have any further thoughts about how to network with other parents, barriers to networking with other parents, or how to overcome stigma about their child's behavior.

Check in to see if parents are having any issues with the playdate process. It might be useful for the clinician to review the steps covered so far, to ask parents how they are feeling about each step, and to ask what remaining questions they have about various steps. The steps (which can be shown on the board or on the flip chart) are as follows:

1 Choosing the right potential friend
2 Helping your child to invite the friend for a playdate
3 Preparing for the playdate to prevent boredom and conflict
4 Teaching your child good friendship skills
5 Intervening in the playdate if boredom and conflict are starting to occur
6 Debriefing with your child after the playdate
7 Preparing your child for a playdate as a guest

"This is our last session. We've covered a lot of things together. Today, we will talk about some issues that might arise in the future and how to prepare for them, and say goodbye."

Note to clinicians: The timing today is more flexible to allow for time to discuss issues from previous sessions that are relevant to parents or to do any video recording reviews that did not fit in previous sessions.

DOI: 10.4324/9781003221715-12

Notes for Group Format
At this time, parents sometimes indicate a desire to trade contact information and/or to continue meeting in the future. We have not initiated this idea ourselves, because we do not want to put pressure on parents to do this if they do not want to. The clinician should consider the unique dynamics of their particular group of parents. However, our inclination has usually been to encourage parents to keep in contact with one another after the session in whatever way feels comfortable and useful for them. One option is that parents can let the clinician know if they would like the clinician to share their contact information with other parents in the group; if so, the clinician can add them to a list that they distribute to all group members who opted in. (This is to take pressure off of parents who may prefer to not share their information.)

2 Deciding Whether to Have another Playdate

Section goal: Parents should judge how the children got along in deciding whether to pursue future playdates. Parents need to weigh their own judgment with what their child wants. Watch out for: Some parents and children will be in conflict about whether or not to have a second playdate.

"Now that your child has had a playdate with a peer, in this section, we will discuss how you decide whether to have another playdate with the same peer or to invite a different one."

"Particularly if it is a new peer, after the playdate is over, you can ask your child in private whether your child would like to get together with the other child again." If the family has had a playdate with a new peer since the start of the PFC program, the clinician can check in now about whether the parent thinks the child is interested in having another playdate with this peer, and whether the parent agrees with the child's opinion about it. The clinician can use this information to shape the focus of the rest of this section.

"In deciding whether to have another playdate with the same peer, parents should use their own judgment to determine:"

- Whether the children have common interests
- Whether the children get along and have fun
- Whether the peer is someone who you want your child to be around (e.g., they bring out good behavior in one other, or at the least, they don't bring out bad behavior)

"What do you do if you and your child are in conflict—for instance, say your child doesn't want to have another playdate but you think this was a good choice?" Ask parents to generate ideas. There aren't clear right and wrong rules; some guiding principles are as follows:

- If you want your child to give the peer another chance, consider having the peer over to your house and make sure to plan something super fun. If your child still doesn't want to pursue the friendship after that, you might have to drop it.
- Try to find out why your child doesn't want to get together again with this peer. Is it because they perceive the peer to not be popular? If so, then you can talk to talk to your child about this. Or does your child say that the peer is mean in private, even if you haven't seen it happen? In that case, your child may have a good reason for not wanting to be friends.

"What about vice versa, if your child wants to have another playdate, but you don't think it's a good choice?" Some suggestions to guide discussion:

- Make a deal to have one or two playdates with someone else, and then if your child still wants to invite that other peer, then they can.
- The exception to this is if the peer puts your child in danger. Then, say no and explain why to your child, using active listening to validate your child's side.

Remind parents about the discussion in the last session about why, in general, it's a good idea for your child to have more than one friend and to have playdates with different peers. Here are the main points:

- One day if the first peer is not available (e.g., moved, on vacation, not interested in being friends with your child any longer), your child has other options.
- Your child gets used to getting along with different types of kids. This prepares your child better for adolescence and adulthood where your child will have to adapt to working with many different types of people.
- If you keep having playdates with one peer, at some point if it is going well, the friend's parents will probably start inviting your child over. This is a great step, but you have to be sure your child is prepared to behave well at the friend's house because you will have less control over antecedents, consequences, and interventions there.

Notes for Group Format

It can be helpful to poll parents to get a quick sense of the consensus in the room so that the clinician knows where to focus. For instance, the clinician can take a poll using a show of hands: "Of the parents who have had playdates with new peers, how many of you think your child would say yes? How many of you think your child would say no? How many of you disagree with your child's opinion about it?"

3 How to Understand another Family's Response to Your Playdate Invitation

Section goal: To present some unspoken rules of parents socializing with each other in the context of playdates. Watch out for: This section may highlight the misattributions of parents with social anxiety, ADHD, rejection histories, or stigma about their child's behavior.

"This is another issue that comes up for families sometimes. In the ideal situation, you and your child select a peer to invite over for a playdate and the other family accepts your invitation. Your child and the peer have a good time and want to get together again. At that point, you might invite over the peer again, and the other family accepts that invitation. Or, the other family might invite your child over for a playdate the next time, which you would accept. It is considered polite for families to more or less 'trade-off hosting playdates', although this isn't a hard-and-fast rule where if you have invited the peer over the first time, the peer must invite your child over next before the two of you can get together again."

"However, things don't always go exactly like that. Now we are going to talk about other responses that the other family might have to your invitations. In each scenario, think about how you would go about determining if this other family is just not interested in the friendship at this time (so it's time to give up and try another family), or if you should keep trying with the same family."

Scenario #1: "You and your child invite a peer for a playdate, but the peer's parents say their family has something else already planned that day. Two weeks later, you invite the same peer again, and the parents say that the weekend you have identified is really busy for them already and they are really sorry. They do sound sorry. What do you do now?"

Open the discussion up to parents. There aren't hard-and-fast rules for what to do in this scenario, and the norms about what to do may vary by the neighborhood and culture of the family. However, here are suggestions that parents have offered in the past:

- If you've invited the other family twice already and they've said no, probably don't invite again until they've invited you to something.
- They may sound sorry when they turn you down, but they could also take the initiative to suggest another date that would work better for them. If they don't do that, it could be time to let it go and move on to finding a different peer to invite.
- You might happen to overhear that the other family is having playdates with other people in the neighborhood (or on the team). If they are (and saying no to your playdates), then this is probably a message.
- If you think they have a believable reason for being sorry, like the parent says the child is in a play that is opening in two months and this is why they are so busy now, but after then would be great, then perhaps after two months you could approach again with a tentative

statement such as "When things settle down, at some point, my child would still like to get together." If the other parent says something vague like "Sure, that would be great," then say something equally vague like "Great, let's touch base whenever it's convenient for you." If the other parent doesn't follow-up, don't bring it up again.

- Don't be upset about being turned down. It might be nothing personal. Even if it is personal, being upset about it is not going to help your child to make friends. Try to forget about it and move on to making connections with a different family.

Scenario #2: "You and your child have had a peer over three times now over the course of two months and the friend has always come, but that family has never invited your child to anything. The children get along and have fun together. What do you do now?"

Here are guidelines that parents have offered in the past:

- Consider whether this other parent is just very busy with a pressing work schedule, many children, caring for an older relative, or something like that. This might explain why they don't reciprocate often. The parent may be grateful for your help.
- However, if you think you are being used for free babysitting, or only as a last resort, then you should put a stop to this.
- If the other parent takes a long time to get back to you about whether they can make the playdate, or cancels at the last minute (and you suspect it's because something better has come up), then be more suspicious.
- But if the other parent accepts right away, seems delighted to have their child come over, is appreciative that you are getting the children together, and states that their child likes yours, then you might be less concerned.

Notes for Group Format

We also find the group format to be particularly useful in this section. It can be better for parents to hear information from other parents about how to react and interpret another family's response than it is to hear this information from the clinician. We rely on the wisdom and support of other group members in the discussion of this topic.

4 Parting Gift

Section goal: For parents to identify something to devote continued work on; to gain closure and wrap up the PFC program. Watch out for: Parents who have difficulty with the ending.

The clinician can express appreciation and respect for the effort that the parent has put into the program. We often say something like, "you deserve a lot of credit for having the commitment and courage to work on your child's behavior and your relationship with your child. You have made a tremendous effort, and your child is incredibly lucky to have a parent who is willing to go the extra mile like this."

Introduce the final exercise. "The PFC program is finished, and as a parting exercise, I would like you to think and reflect about what you will do during the time that you would have been coming to session. While it is easy to forget about that quickly and let the time get filled by other things, I hope that you will find some way to continue to use this time to support your child and to improve the gains you have seen."

Ask parents to reflect upon and state how they might use this time in future weeks to continue working on the friendship skills and reinforce the gains they have seen with their children.

Notes for Group Format
Sometimes this section takes quite a bit of time in group format, because parents have grown close and wish to offer words of encouragement to one another. While keeping time constraints in mind, we usually encourage this.

5 Ending Business

Hand out the final Parent Satisfaction form (optional) and collect these sheets when parents have completed them. Thank parents for their participation and wish them well.

Notes for Group Format
The Parent Satisfaction form may be more useful if PFC is being delivered in group format.

Appendix A: Intervention Fidelity Checklists

Session 1 Understanding Your Child's Social Behaviors

Intervention Fidelity Checklist

Date: _____ Clinician: _____

1 **Clinician and Parent Introductions**
   - ❑ Clinician introduced themselves and explained their background
   - ❑ Clinician presented the history and rationale of PFC
   - ❑ Clinician went over the PFC Pyramid (Handout 1.1) and the Outline of Topics (Handout 1.2)

2 **Thinking about Your Child's Social Problems**
   - ❑ Clinician introduced Common Social Behaviors Displayed by Children with ADHD (Handout 1.3)
   - ❑ Clinician led a discussion about children's social behaviors

3 **Antecedents, Behavior, Consequences (ABC) Model**
   - ❑ Clinician presented the ABC model (Handout 1.4)
   - ❑ Clinician led activities/discussion about the ABC model
   - ❑ Clinician presented Homework 1.1 (ABC model)

4 **Special Time**
   - ❑ Clinician introduced and presented Special Time (Handout 1.5)
   - ❑ Clinician led activities/discussion about Special Time
   - ❑ Clinician presented Homework 1.2 (Special Time Practice)

5 **Ending Business**
   - ❑ Clinician reminded the parent about homework
   - ❑ Parent completed the Parent Satisfaction form

Session 2 Giving Effective Feedback to
Your Child about Social Behaviors

Intervention Fidelity Checklist

Date: _____ Clinician: _____

1 **Review of Homework**
   ❏ Clinician checked in about homework

2 **How to Talk so Kids Will Listen and Listen so Kids Will Talk**
   ❏ Clinician presented the main points about active listening (Handout 2.1)
   ❏ Clinician led activities/discussion about active listening
   ❏ Clinician presented Homework 2.1 (Practice Active Listening)

3 **Using Praise and Corrective Feedback, Part 1**
   ❏ Clinician presented the main points about praise and corrections (Handout 2.2)
   ❏ Clinician led activities/discussion about praise and corrective feedback
   ❏ Clinician presented Homework 2.2 (Praise Practice) and 2.3 (Keep up Special Time)

4 **Ending Business**
   ❏ Clinician reminded the parent about homework
   ❏ Parent completed the Parent Satisfaction form

PARENTAL
FRIENDSHIP
COACHING

Session 3 Helping Your Child to Choose the Right Friends

Intervention Fidelity Checklist

Date: _____ Clinician: _____

1 Review of Homework
- ☐ Clinician checked in about homework

2 Using Praise and Corrective Feedback, Part 2
- ☐ Clinician presented the main points about giving effective corrective feedback (Handout 3.1)
- ☐ Clinician led activities/discussion about corrective feedback
- ☐ Clinician presented Homework 3.1 (Praise and Corrective Feedback)

3 Video Recording Review (Optional)
- ☐ Clinician played video provided by the parent to illustrate a parent–child, or child–friend, interaction
- ☐ Clinician and parent discussed the video

4 Choosing a Good Friend for a Playdate
- ☐ Clinician presented the main points about choosing friends (Handouts 3.2 and 3.3)
- ☐ Clinician led activities/discussion about choosing a good friend
- ☐ Clinician presented Homework 3.2 (Choosing a Friend for a Playdate)
- ☐ Clinicians presented Homework 3.3 (Continue Relationship Building)

5 Ending Business
- ☐ Clinician reminded the parent about homework
- ☐ Parent completed the Parent Satisfaction form

PARENTAL
FRIENDSHIP
COACHING

Session 4   Preparing for a Playdate as a Host, Part 1

Intervention Fidelity Checklist

Date: _____ Clinician: _____

1   Review of Homework
- ❏ Clinician checked in about homework

2   How to Handle Oppositional Behavior against Parental Guidance
- ❏ Clinician presented the main points about handling oppositional and argumentative behaviors (Handout 4.1)
- ❏ Clinician led activities/discussion about handling oppositional and argumentative behaviors
- ❏ Clinician presented Homework 4.1 (Handling Oppositional Behavior Practice)

3   Video Recording Review (Optional)
- ❏ Clinician played video provided by the parent to illustrate a parent–child, or child–friend, interaction
- ❏ Clinician and parent discussed the video

4   Preventing Boredom and Conflict during a Playdate, Part 1
- ❏ Clinician presented the main points about preventing boredom and conflict on playdates (Handout 4.2)
- ❏ Clinician led activities/discussion about preventing boredom and conflict and being a good host
- ❏ Clinician presented the main points about talking to a peer about what to do on a playdate (Handout 4.3)
- ❏ Clinician led activities/discussion about talking to a peer about what to do on a playdate
- ❏ Clinician presented Homework 4.2 (Practice Talking with a Peer about What to Do on a playdate)
- ❏ Clinicians presented Homework 4.3 (Continue Relationship-Building)

5   Ending Business
- ❏ Clinician reminded the parent about homework
- ❏ Parent completed the Parent Satisfaction form

Session 5 Teaching Your Child Social Skills, Part 1

Intervention Fidelity Checklist

Date: _____ Clinician: _____

1 **Review of Homework**
   ☐ Clinician checked in about homework

2 **Video Recording Review (Optional)**
   ☐ Clinician played video provided by the parent to illustrate a parent–child, or child–friend, interaction
   ☐ Clinician and parent discussed the video

3 **Helping Your Child Learn Good Friendship Skills, Part 1**
   ☐ Clinician presented the main points about helping children improve game-playing skills (Handout 5.1)
   ☐ Clinician led activities/discussion about helping children improve game-playing skills
   ☐ Clinician presented Homework 5.1 (Game Skills Practice)

4 **Preventing Boredom and Conflict during a Playdate, Part 2**
   ☐ Clinician presented the main points about being a good host (Handout 5.2)
   ☐ Clinician led activities/discussion about being a good host
   ☐ Clinician presented Homework 5.2 (Continue Relationship-Building)

5 **Ending Business**
   ☐ Clinician reminded the parent about homework
   ☐ Parent completed the Parent Satisfaction form

PARENTAL
FRIENDSHIP
COACHING

Session 6 Preparing for a Playdate as a Host, Part 2

Intervention Fidelity Checklist

Date: _____ Clinician: _____

1 **Review of Homework**
   ☐ Clinician checked in about homework

2 **Helping Your Child Learn Good Friendship Skills, Part 2**
   ☐ Clinician presented the main points of conversational skills (Handouts 6.1 and 6.2)
   ☐ Clinician led activities/discussion about conversational skills
   ☐ Clinician presented Homework 6.1 (Practice Conversational Skills)

3 **Handling Boredom and Conflict during the Playdate when Best Efforts Fail**
   ☐ Clinician presented the main points of instructing child during a playdate (Handout 6.3)
   ☐ Clinician led activities/discussion about handling problem behavior during a playdate
   ☐ Clinician presented Homework 6.2 (Continue Relationship-Building)

4 **Video Recording Review (Optional)**
   ☐ Clinician played video provided by the parent to illustrate a parent–child, or child–friend, interaction
   ☐ Clinician and parent discussed the video

5 **Ending Business**
   ☐ Clinician reminded the parent about homework
   ☐ Parent completed the Parent Satisfaction form

Session 7 Teaching Your Child Social Skills, Part 2

Intervention Fidelity Checklist

Date: _____ Clinician: _____

1 **Review of Homework**
   - ❑ Clinician checked in about homework

2 **Helping Your Child Learn Good Friendship Skills, Part 3**
   - ❑ Clinician presented the main points of dealing with negative emotions in children (Handout 7.1)
   - ❑ Clinician led activities/discussion about dealing with negative emotions
   - ❑ Clinician presented Homework 7.1 (Practice Dealing with Negative Emotions)

3 **Giving Effective Feedback after the Playdate**
   - ❑ Clinician presented the main points of debriefing after a playdate (Handout 7.2)
   - ❑ Clinician led activities/discussion about debriefing after a playdate
   - ❑ Clinician presented Homework 7.2 (Continue Relationship-Building)

4 **Video Recording Review (Optional)**
   - ❑ Clinician played video provided by the parent to illustrate a parent–child, or child–friend, interaction
   - ❑ Clinician and parent discussed the video

5 **Ending Business**
   - ❑ Clinician reminded the parent about homework
   - ❑ Parent completed the Parent Satisfaction form

Session 8 Preparing for a Playdate as a Guest

Intervention Fidelity Checklist

Date: _____ Clinician: _____

1 **Review of Homework**
   ❑ Clinician checked in about homework

2 **Preparing for a Playdate as a Guest**
   ❑ Clinician presented the main points of preparing the child to be a guest (Handouts 8.1 and 8.2)
   ❑ Clinician led activities/discussion about preparing the child to be a guest

3 **Picking Up Your Child from a Playdate as a Guest**
   ❑ Clinician presented the main points of picking up child from a playdate (Handout 8.3)
   ❑ Clinician led activities/discussion about picking up child from a playdate
   ❑ Clinician presented Homework 8.1 (Continue Relationship-Building)

4 **Video Recording Review (Optional)**
   ❑ Clinician played video provided by the parent to illustrate a parent–child, or child–friend, interaction
   ❑ Clinician and parent discussed the video

5 **Ending Business**
   ❑ Clinician reminded the parent about homework
   ❑ Parent completed the Parent Satisfaction form

Session 9 Meeting New Peers

Intervention Fidelity Checklist

Date: _____ Clinician: _____

1 **Review of Homework**
   ❑ Clinician checked in about homework

2 **Meeting New Friends**
   ❑ Clinician presented the main points about meeting new friends (Handouts 9.1 and 9.2)
   ❑ Clinician led activities/discussion about meeting new friends

3 **Parent-to-Parent Networking**
   ❑ Clinician presented the main points about networking with other parents (Handout 9.3)
   ❑ Clinician led activities/discussion about networking with other parents
   ❑ Clinician presented Homework 9.1 (Meeting New Peers)
   ❑ Clinician presented Homework 9.2 (Continue Relationship-Building)

4 **Video Recording Review (Optional)**
   ❑ Clinician played video provided by the parent to illustrate a parent–child, or child–friend, interaction
   ❑ Clinician and parent discussed the video

5 **Ending Business**
   ❑ Clinician reminded the parent about homework
   ❑ Parent completed the Parent Satisfaction form

Session 10 Getting Ready for the Future

Intervention Fidelity Checklist

Date: _____ Clinician: _____

1 **Review of Homework**
   ❑ Clinician checked in about homework

2 **Deciding Whether to Have another Playdate**
   ❑ Clinician presented the main points about deciding whether to pursue future playdates
   ❑ Clinician led activities/discussion about deciding whether to pursue future playdates

3 **How to Understand another Family's Response to Your Playdate Invitation**
   ❑ Clinician presented the main points about understanding another family's response
   ❑ Clinician led activities/discussion about understanding another family's response

4 **Parting Gift**
   ❑ Clinician acknowledged parents' commitment and courage
   ❑ Clinician led a discussion about the "gift of time"

5 **Ending Business**
   ❑ Parent completed the Parent Satisfaction form

Appendix B: Parent Handouts

Session 1 Topics

1 Introductions
2 Thinking about Your Child's Social Problems
3 Antecedents, Behavior, Consequences (ABC) Model
4 Special Time
5 Ending Business

The PFC Pyramid

Handout 1.1

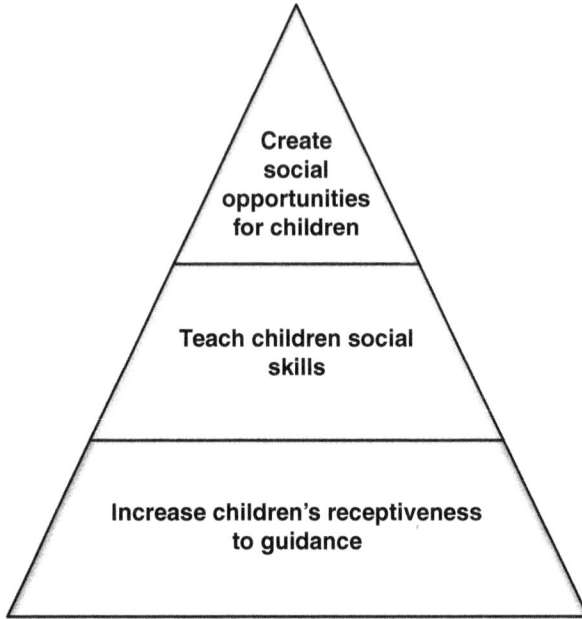

Outline of Topics

Handout 1.2

Welcome to the Parental Friendship Coaching, or PFC, program! Parenting a child with ADHD is a challenging job. The goal in this program is to promote your children's friendships and social skills and to support happy parent–child relationships in the process. I aim to do this by providing you with tools and techniques that can assist you in being a "friendship coach" for your child.

The program includes 10 sessions for parents. Each session covers different topics. I will ask that you try out the strategies at home with your child between each meeting. The more the parents carry out the homework, the more they get out of the program. So, I strongly encourage you to do the homework and to attend every session.

I want you to take an active role in the program. Please ask questions if you do not understand something or need a little more assistance with any topic or area of concern. Once again, welcome! I am so pleased that you are here, and hope you and your child find benefit in participating in this program.

Session 1 Understanding Your Child's Social Behaviors
Session 2 Giving Effective Feedback to Your Child about Social Behaviors
Session 3 Helping Your Child to Choose the Right Friends
Session 4 Preparing for a Playdate as a Host, Part 1
Session 5 Teaching Your Child Social Skills, Part 1
Session 6 Preparing for a Playdate as a Host, Part 2
Session 7 Teaching Your Child Social Skills, Part 2
Session 8 Preparing for a Playdate as a Guest
Session 9 Meeting New Peers
Session 10 Getting Ready for the Future

Common Social Behaviors Displayed by Children with ADHD

Handout 1.3

Negative social behaviors related to inattention

Appears apathetic, uninterested in the activities	YES	NO
Daydreams, drifts off	YES	NO
Sluggish, slow to respond to peers in verbal back-and-forth interchanges	YES	NO
Can't remember rules of a game or what somebody said	YES	NO
Doesn't ask other people questions or join in the conversation	YES	NO
Misses social cues like that peer is tired, wants to leave, is feeling sad	YES	NO
Disorganized, messy, can't find toys or materials for play	YES	NO

Negative social behaviors related to hyperactivity/impulsivity

Monopolizes conversation, talks too much, doesn't let others talk	YES	NO
Talks about self or own interests when peers are clearly not interested	YES	NO
Interrupts peers when in a conversation	YES	NO
Intrudes into activities, barges in, doesn't wait for a break in the game	YES	NO
Monopolizes activities, acts as if peer is a "play slave" who must obey and go along	YES	NO
Is a bad winner or bad loser, gloats when wins, or complains and gets upset when loses	YES	NO
Cheats at games, rearranges the rules to own advantage	YES	NO
Changes the subject to something new in a way that is not skillful	YES	NO

Other common social problems in children with ADHD

Drawn to the wrong friends (troublemakers)	YES	NO
Doesn't like the types of games or activities that most other children like to do	YES	NO
Oversensitive, has trouble responding to minor teasing	YES	NO
Gets into trouble with adults (teachers, adult supervisors of activities)	YES	NO
Has a bad reputation at school	YES	NO
Has social anxiety, gets nervous when meeting new peers	YES	NO

Positive social behaviors and strengths of your child (checklist)

____ Kind-hearted and warm, compassionate
____ Spontaneous
____ Fun-loving, often cheerful
____ Excellent sense of humor
____ Good at games (sports, common board games kids like)
____ Well-liked by adults
____ Does well once other kids really get to know them
____ Friendly and welcoming to new kids
____ Bold and unafraid to try new things or meet new kids
____ Authentic and honest
____ Will persevere and keep trying
____ Other strengths (please write below)

The Antecedents, Behavior, Consequences
(ABC) Model Worksheet

Handout 1.4

Identify one to three undesirable behaviors your child shows with peers and write them in the "behavior" section. Write down the current antecedents that are encouraging each behavior. Finally, write down the current consequences that come to your child for each behavior. "Nothing" may also be a consequence.

A *Antecedents*	B *Behavior*	C *Consequences*

Write some possible ideas for ways to change antecedents or consequences to reduce the likelihood of the undesirable behavior occurring.

_____
_____
_____
_____
_____

Special Time

Handout 1.5

Special Time is a time for your child to experience positive attention from you. This is not a reward for a behavior that your child has performed; instead, it is a special time that you have regularly to build your relationship together.

1 **Set up Special Time for 15 minutes, several days a week.** You can schedule a regular time that is to become your Special Time every day, or you can find a time each day as it arises.
2 **It is best if nobody else except you and your child are involved.** Put siblings elsewhere or with another adult. If there are two parents in the family, each parent might do a separate Special Time with the child if they want to.
3 **At the beginning of Special Time, ask your child what they would like to play or talk about.** You can make suggestions (see list to follow).
4 **Let your child take the lead.** Do not take control of the play activity or topic of conversation.
5 **Younger children: Describe what they are doing while playing.** It is something like a sportscaster calling the plays of a game. If your child is drawing, this might sound something like: "It looks like you are drawing green grass. Now, you are adding red and yellow flowers. It looks like a garden." (If you are wrong, your child will correct you. Don't argue with your child about what it is. Just continue on with the information your child provides.) Use an animated and action-oriented tone of voice. It is all right to ask questions to clarify your child's play if you are not sure what they are doing. Most children like this kind of attention from a parent. You are showing your child that you find their play activity interesting.
6 **Older children: Listen attentively and ask questions to learn more about their expertise while having a conversation.** It is something like a talk show host (such as Oprah) interviewing a guest of honor who the host likes and respects. The talk show host genuinely wants to encourage the guest to tell their story and is sympathetic toward the guest. For example, if your child is explaining a video game to you, you might listen attentively and respectfully, and sometimes ask questions about who the child's favorite character is and why, or what was the most challenging level to learn how to get through. You are showing your child that you are interested in their interests.
7 **Do not teach, command, correct, criticize, or give instructions during Special Time.** Avoid the temptation to "teach" your child how to do something during this Special Time or to take over your child's play activity. This is your child's time to show you something that they are interested in or the expert about.

8   **Relax and enjoy your child!** This is a time for you and your child to get to know each other better without conflict.

9   **Ignore mild misbehavior**. If the misbehavior is not too bad, try to ignore it. One reason why Special Time is only 10 or 15 minutes is because, depending on your child, it may be unrealistic to ignore mild misbehavior for longer than that. If your child is misbehaving severely, you may say calmly you will play later when they can play nicely and then leave the room. If your child becomes extremely aggressive or destructive, discipline your child as you might normally do. Resume Special Time when your child has settled down.

10   **This is not easy to do at first!** Many parents make mistakes during the first few times, usually by giving too many commands. Many parents also feel awkward at first. Don't worry! Just keep practicing, and this will become easy to do.

NOTE: Although Special Time is designed to be spent with the child who has behavior problems, if there are siblings who would want (and benefit from) their own Special Time, you can plan separate Special Time periods with each child if you like.

Activity Suggestions For Special Time

Younger children (ages 6–8)

Beyblades, Barbies, Legos©
Play-doh, Clay
Crayons, paints (watercolors), colored chalk, markers
Drawing paper
Coloring book
Plastic figurines, action characters, soldiers
Sandbox, dirt
Family of puppets
Dollhouse and family
Baby doll with a baby bottle and/or other accessories
Building materials: Tinker toys, blocks, Legos©
Toy cars
Toy animals, stuffed animals
Fantasy play, dress up, imagination games
Building blocks
Sculpturing clay
Puzzles, 3D puzzles
Model cars/planes/boats

Older children (ages 9–11)

Sculpturing clay
Puzzles, 3D puzzles
Model cars/planes/boats (should be simple enough so parent doesn't need
    to be directive and correct mistakes)
Building material: wood, hammer and nails, sets of building blocks
Science equipment: chemistry set, ecological set
Sports: Basketball, batting cages, miniature golf
Kicking around a ball (as long as it is not an organized game where the
    parent will require the child to follow the rules)
Simple cooking or baking (if it will not require the parent to be too dir-
    ective and the parent can go with the flow, even if the child is making
    mistakes)
Decorating cookies, cupcakes
Talking about anything the parent usually isn't interested in hearing about
    (e.g., one child liked to talk about video games with their parent who
    usually wasn't very interested.)

**It is less important what activity you do and more important that you interact
with your child in a way that shows interest in what your child cares about,
lets your child take the lead, and does not include correction or teaching.**

PARENTAL
FRIENDSHIP
COACHING

Session 1 Homework List

Homework 1.1	ABC Model
	Complete Handout 1.4. observe your child's social relationships and start thinking about one antecedent and one consequence that can be reinforcing the behavior. Bring the handout back next session.
Date	Observations (child reactions, successes, obstacles, etc.)
Homework 1.2	Special Time Practice
	Try to find 10–15 minutes two or three times this week to do Special Time with your child. For some families, it is easier to do one longer activity that is 45 minutes once per week. Generally speaking though, more times per week (even if a shorter amount for each time) is better than one longer activity.
Date	Observations (child reactions, successes, obstacles, etc.)

Session 1 Parent Satisfaction Form

How useful did you find the session this week (circle one)?

1----------2----------3----------4----------5----------6----------7
Not at all   Medium   Very much

Comments, questions, or suggestions:

Name: _____

Thank you for your honest feedback; it helps me better serve your needs and helps to improve the sessions for future parents.

Session 2 Topics

1   **Review of Homework**
2   **How to Listen so Kids Will Talk**
3   **Using Praise and Corrective Feedback, Part 1**
4   **Ending Business**

How to Listen so Kids Will Talk

Handout 2.1

Try to find a time when you can ask your child about their social life.

Possible times to talk

- After a playdate that you have observed
- After the child comes home from school or an activity (better if you have observed it)
- Before bedtime as a check-in about the day
- In the car
- While cooking (if the cooking does not require too much attention)
- While taking a walk
- When your child seems upset, annoyed, or put out about something (keep a lookout for a time when your child seems upset about a social interaction that has happened, perhaps a fight with a peer or an experience of being teased)
- After you have observed a negative peer interaction that you think probably made your child feel badly
- Any time that is quiet, private between you and your child, and you can focus your attention on your child (e.g., don't do this when you are trying to get your child and siblings ready for school on time)
- Any time when your child doesn't have something else they want to do immediately (e.g., don't try to do this when their favorite TV show is starting, or your child is too tired to focus on the conversation)

Possible conversation leads to open (and continue) the discussion

- "Tell me one good thing and one bad thing that happened today" (some families ask "what was the rainbow and what was the raincloud" or some other term for the good and the bad).
- "What is something nice someone did for you today?"
- "What is something nice you did for someone else?"
- "What did you play today at recess?"
- "How did you feel about playing with the other children?"
- "Did anything make you smile today? Did anything make you sad or mad?"
- "Who would you say is your friend?"
- "What do you like to do with Maddie" (younger kids)? "What do you like about Maddie" (older kids)?
- "Do you ever feel lonely at (school/activity)?"
- "You and David used to play together a lot, but I haven't seen him over much lately. What happened?" "How are you feeling about that?"
- "How is your friend Linelle? You seem to really like her."
- "You seemed to have fun today playing with the Connect Four." "What do you think made that so fun?"

- "You seem sort of down today. Want to talk about it?"
- "It seems like maybe that hurt your feelings when Jazmin wouldn't let you play."

During the discussion, try to do these behaviors
- Empathize
- Be attentive
- Give the impression that what your child says is really important
- Give the impression that you really care about what your child is saying (remember nonverbal cues and tone of voice as well as verbal ones)
- Take what your child says seriously; avoid accusing your child of lying
- Focus on your child's feelings (especially if anger, sadness, and frustration) and don't get caught up in the exact details of who said what and what exactly happened
- Restate what your child says (as much as it still feels natural to do so)
- If your child is upset, be comforting
- Ask your child how they feel about that
- Avoid (at this point) giving solutions or problem-solving
- Try to not interrupt
- Avoid directing the conversation (much)
- Avoid criticism and judgment
- Avoid asking too many questions; you don't want this to feel like an inquisition
- It's okay for there to be pauses in the conversation, periods of quiet where you just wait for your child to think things through, or hug your child

Remember to spend at least 10 minutes on active listening before jumping into giving your child suggestions for how to solve the problem or what to do better next time.

PARENTAL
FRIENDSHIP
COACHING

Giving Effective Praise to Children

Handout 2.2

Praise is a powerful way to shape your child's behavior and build your relationship with your child in the process. Children can feel put down if praise is not tactful, however. In general, with younger children, you should be more dramatic, louder, and effusive (ham it up!), and with older children, you should be more subdued when giving praise (but still seem genuine, proud, and glowing). Here's how to tactfully praise:

A **Eye contact**: Look your child in the eye and make sure you have their attention (important for kids with ADHD).

B **Body language**: Move as close to your child as the situation will allow. Pulling the child aside to give praise is more effective than shouting it out in front of their playmates. Younger children may not mind as much if other people overhear the praise, but older children tend to be more embarrassed.

C **Voice tone**: Clearly audible and slightly warm for older children (about ages 9–11), or very warm and effusive for younger children (about ages 6–8). Older children are more sensitive to the idea that you are treating them like a baby.

D **Content**: Make it short, but say exactly what your child did that you liked (see examples of effective praise below).

E **Timing**: Don't wait for the perfect behavior to praise. Start with 30% perfect. Try to give the praise as soon as possible after the positive behavior occurred. However, if your child is easily embarrassed (or older), you may have to wait until you are in private to give the praise.

F **Avoid discouraging statements**: See examples of ineffective praise below. Also avoid comparing your child to others, even if the comparison is positive, e.g., "You're much better at sharing than your brother is." It will set up competition and rivalry. Instead say, "You are terrific at sharing."

Effective praise (specific to friendship and social skills)

1 Your playroom looks very clean and tidy!
2 Playing friendly with Matthew makes me very happy.
3 What a terrific job you did sharing your models with Julio.
4 I like the way you let Desiree choose the game because she is your guest.
5 You have such a pretty smile.
6 It's so helpful when you put everything away after you are finished playing!
7 You really showed good cooperating when you let Lin go first.
8 Great job on being a good sport even when you lost the game.
9 Thank you for putting away your toys when I asked.
10 You made a super effort at ignoring Britney's teasing.

Ineffective praise

1 Why can't your playroom look like this all the time?
2 That sure beats how you usually treat Matthew.
3 You finally shared your models with Julio, but why did you have that grumpy look on your face?
4 I wish you could let your guests choose like this more often.
5 Is that a smile or a smirk?
6 Your cards are picked up, but I see one of your checkers over there.
7 Great job cooperating today, but I think you annoyed Lin by talking too much.
8 You managed to keep your temper when you lost today, but most kids your age are mature enough so they don't have to work on this.
9 You put away your toys when I asked you, but I shouldn't have to ask.
10 You ignored Britney's teasing right now. I just hope you don't get back at her when I am away.

99 Ways to Say "Very Good"

1   You're on the right track!
2   Such a good job!
3   You did a lot of work today!
4   You remembered!
5   Now you have the hang of it!
6   You make it look easy.
7   That's the way!
8   Couldn't have done it better myself!
9   Sensational!
10   That's the best you have ever done.
11   You're really working hard today.
12   You are learning fast.
13   Amazing work.
14   Well look at you go!
15   Exactly right!
16   You're really improving.
17   You outdid yourself today.
18   You are really learning a lot.
19   You're really going to town!
20   You did that very well.
21   You've got it made.
22   Keep up the good work.
23   You're getting better every day.
24   That's quite good.
25   That's very much better!
26   Good for you!
27   Congratulations!
28   I'm happy to see you working like that.
29   You are very good at that.
30   Excellent progress.
31   That's quite an accomplishment.
32   Good going!
33   Nothing can stop you now!
34   Wonderful!
35   Nice going.
36   I've never seen you do it better.
37   Well look at that!
38   Incredible job.
39   That kind of work makes me very happy.
40   Superb!
41   Keep it up!
42   Wow!!!!
43   Perfect!
44   You're doing beautifully.

45   I'm proud of the way you worked today.
46   You really make my job fun.
47   I like that.
48   That was first class.
49   Outstanding!!!
50   You've got it now.
51   That's great.
52   You've got your brain in gear today!
53   That's it!
54   You've just about got it.
55   High five!
56   You must have been practicing.
57   Good remembering!
58   Keep it up!
59   Good work!
60   Now you've figured it out.
61   That's better than ever.
62   Tremendous!!
63   Right on!
64   You are doing that much better today.
65   Marvelous!!
66   Good job, (name of child).
67   I'm very proud of you.
68   Terrific!
69   Woo-hoo!
70   Now you've figured it out.
71   That's really nice.
72   Hey hey, look at you!
73   That's the right way to do it.
74   Nice going.
75   You've just about mastered that!
76   Now that's what I call a fine job.
77   You did it!
78   I knew you could do it.
79   You rock.
80   That's the best ever.
81   That's better!
82   Great work!
83   Fantastic!
84   You've got that down pat.
85   You certainly did well today.
86   Congratulations!
87   You figured that out fast.
88   That's coming along nicely.
89   Terrific!
90   That's right!

91   That's the way to do it!
92   You haven't missed a thing.
93   One more time and you'll have it.
94   Super dooper.
95   Excellent!
96   Now you have it!
97   Oh yeah!
98   Mighty fine!
99   That's wonderful!

PARENTAL
FRIENDSHIP
COACHING

Session 2 Homework List

Homework 2.1	Practice Active Listening
	Try to use more active listening skills with your child at least once. You might be able to build it into Special Time.
Date	**Observations** (child reactions, successes, obstacles, etc.)

Homework 2.2	Praise Practice
	Try praising your child about a social interaction/social behavior you observed. Remember that you may need to praise the part that is correct even if the rest is not correct. *Try to keep it separate from your Homework 2.1 conversation*—the good part about active listening is that it is supposed to be nondirective and nonevaluative (like Special Time). Kids like that; don't "spoil" active listening by jumping in and starting to be directive and solution-oriented.
Date	**Observations** (child reactions, successes, obstacles, etc.)

Homework 2.3	Keep up Special Time
	Keep trying Special Time. You can probably build Homework 2.1 about active listening into one of the sessions of Special Time.
Date	**Observations** (child reactions, successes, obstacles, etc.)

Session 2 Parent Satisfaction Form

Did you complete your homework assignments over the previous week?

Homework 1.1: Complete Handout 1.4 about your child's behavior with a peer (ABC Model)
Yes   No

Homework 1.2: Try Special Time with your child
Yes   No

Since the last session until today, approximately how much time (if any) did you spend *outside of session* doing homework assignments, thinking about what was discussed, looking over the handouts, or discussing topics from the session with other people?

_____ minutes in total

How useful did you find the session this week (circle one)?

1----------2----------3----------4----------5----------6----------7
Not at all   Medium   Very much

Comments, questions, or suggestions:

Name: _____

Thank you for your honest feedback; it helps me better serve your needs and helps to improve the program for future parents.

Session 3 Topics

1   Review of Homework
2   Using Praise and Corrective Feedback, Part 2
3   Video Recording Review (Optional)
4   Choosing a Good Friend for a Playdate
5   Ending Business

Giving Effective Corrective Feedback to Children

Handout 3.1

Corrective feedback is necessary to shape behavior sometimes, but learning to give it effectively is a real art. When feedback is given effectively, this maximizes the chances that your child will be able to hear it and use it effectively. Children are sensitive to feeling put-down, criticized, or belittled. Here's how to give effective corrective feedback:

A **Eye contact**: Look your child in the eye and make sure you have their attention (important for kids with ADHD).

B **Body language**: Move as close to your child as the situation will allow. Whenever possible, do it in private with your child and not in front of playmates. For example, ask to speak to your child in private, or find a quiet time to check in. Don't shout the feedback across the room (especially if others can hear). Older children are more likely than younger children to be embarrassed by you correcting them in front of other people.

C **Voice tone**: Calm, yet firm. Don't yell or lecture. Try not to get angry or upset. If you stay in emotional control, it makes it more likely your child will stay in control.

D **Content**: Make it short, but say exactly what your child did that was not acceptable. Don't blow it out of proportion by saying "always" and "never" or making this about character traits; stick to concrete behaviors that need correction. Stick to the here and now, and don't bring up a list of other examples from the past (see examples of effective corrective feedback below).

E **Timing**: Ideally, corrective feedback is given as soon after the act as possible. However, if it will embarrass your child to give them feedback in front of other people, you may need to wait until you have a private time. Remember to also find something genuine to praise as well; you want to keep the praise to corrective feedback ratio at least 4:1 if possible.

F **Avoid discouraging statements**: See examples of ineffective corrective feedback below.

Finally, consider **changing the antecedents in the future** so that it reduces the likelihood that you will need to give corrective feedback next time.

Effective corrective feedback (specific to friendship and social skills)

1 Remember to let Jennifer choose the game because she is your guest.

2 I know you are excited about playing this game, but you need to let Hiro have his turn too.

3   You need to be a good sport even when you lose the game. Say "nice job" to the winner.
4   I know it is difficult, but I want you to ignore Shauna's teasing.
5   If you don't want to play any longer, ask your friend if it is okay to switch games.
6   Next time please offer to help your friend put away the toys.
7   I think Avery wants to play with your models. You need to share them with her this time. Next time if you don't want to share them, we will put them away before your friend comes over.
8   I don't know if Sam wants to play that any longer. Why don't you go ask him now what he would like to do?
9   Remember to say nice things to your friend when you win the game. You can say, "good game," and act like winning isn't a big deal to you. (With older children, perhaps: "What would be a nice thing you can say?")
10 Sometimes other children don't like to be told how to play. You need to color your own picture and let Janine color her own picture the way she wants to.

Ineffective corrective feedback

1   You are being selfish by making Jennifer play what you want to play. Last week you did the same thing with Jessica, and look how mad she got. And the time before that too....
2   No wonder Hiro doesn't like you; you hog the game and won't let anybody else have a turn.
3   What a bad sport you are. I didn't raise you like that. You must get that from your father.
4   Who cares if Shauna is teasing you? Can't you lighten up? It's not a big deal!
5   You never ask permission and you can't finish any game. You really need to work on that.
6   Your friend is probably mad because you didn't even offer to help put away the toys. And her mom probably thinks I'm a bad mom for not teaching you manners either.
7   Why can't you share? You should be grateful for everything you have when there are other children less fortunate than yourself out there.
8   Are you making Sam do things he hates again?
9   Nobody likes a gloater and that's what you are.
10 Can't you be more mature, instead of trying to be the boss of every situation? Your teacher says this is a problem for you at school as well.

Common Mistakes Made by Children with ADHD When Choosing Friends

Handout 3.2

Children with ADHD often struggle with reading social cues, so they have more difficulty deciding who would be a good friend. Here are some common mistakes children with ADHD make when choosing friends, and why:

1 **Picking the most popular peer**
   - ❏ Your child may pick the most popular peer in class, not necessarily one who shares common interests with your child or one who seems to like your child.
   - ❏ Children who don't have many friends may do this because they see this as "winning the friendship lottery," and they don't understand that they would not be happy over the long term with this friend.

2 **Picking a meek peer**
   - ❏ Your child may pick the peer who will obey them, whoever is meek enough to let your child boss them around. The friendship is not built on mutual interests.
   - ❏ Children with ADHD, particularly those who don't have many friends, sometimes want their own personal "play slave."

3 **Picking whoever will take them**
   - ❏ Your child may be friends with whoever will accept them as a friend, and sometimes gets taken advantage of because peers will pick your child if they can boss your child around.
   - ❏ Some children are so grateful for attention they don't care who it's from, and so afraid of losing a friend they will do anything. This is dangerous especially as kids get older.

4 **Picking troublemakers**
   - ❏ Your child may be drawn to kids who are always in trouble at school for their behavior.
   - ❏ If your child often gets in trouble, it may make them feel better to have friends who behave as badly or worse. It may also be exciting and flattering to have friends like this.

Qualities to Look for in a Potential Friend

Handout 3.3

The ideal potential friend is a peer who:
- is kind to your child
- has similar interests as your child
- is already inclined to like your child
- your child is already inclined to like them
- brings out good behavior in your child or at least does not bring out bad behavior in your child (and vice versa for your child bringing out good behavior in the peer)
- listens to you and obeys your house rules

Other nice-to-have qualities are that the potential friend might be a peer who:
- is the same age as your child (within about one year)
- is in the same grade as your child
- might be the same gender as your child
- is not related to your child
- goes to the same school as your child
- is in the same classroom as your child

The qualities in the "ideal" list are most important because they are about the character of the friend and how the child and friend get along. If a potential friend fills most of the "ideal" list, let the "nice-to-have" qualities go.

The "nice-to-have" qualities are included because children this age usually have friends who are the same age and gender, so this type of friendship will look more typical to peers. Also, if your child has a good friend in the same school or classroom, this may help your child like school better and help improve the way that other peers there view your child.

Session 3 Homework List

Homework 3.1	Praise and Corrective Feedback
	Continue to try giving more effective praise and corrective feedback to your child.
Date	Observations (child reactions, successes, obstacles, etc.)
Homework 3.2	Choosing a Peer for a Playdate
	Discuss with your child who they might like to invite over for a playdate. Keep in mind what we have talked about today regarding the ideal qualities of a potential friend.
Date	Observations (child reactions, successes, obstacles, etc.)
Homework 3.3	Continue Relationship-Building
	Continue Special Time, active listening, etc. The idea is that these strategies will fade more into the background as they become second-nature.
Date	Observations (child reactions, successes, obstacles, etc.)

Playdate Progress:

For this week, work on arranging a playdate for your child. The skills we have learned so far are as follows:

- With your child, discuss who you would like to invite for a playdate.

Session 3 Parent Satisfaction Form

Did you complete your homework assignments over the previous week?

Homework 2.1: Try Active Listening with your child
Yes   No

Homework 2.2: Try giving more effective praise
Yes   No

Homework 2.3: Continue practicing Special Time (can be done in conjunction with Homework 2.1)
Yes   No

Since the last session until today, approximately how much time (if any) did you spend *outside of session* doing homework assignments, thinking about what was discussed, looking over the handouts, or discussing topics from the session with other people?

_____ minutes in total

How useful did you find the session this week (circle one)?

1----------2----------3----------4----------5----------6----------7
Not at all   Medium   Very much

Comments, questions, or suggestions:

Name: _____

Thank you for your honest feedback; it helps me better serve your needs and helps to improve the program for future parents.

Session 4 Topics

1 Review of Homework
2 How to Handle Oppositional Behavior against Parental Guidance
3 Video Recording Review (Optional)
4 Preventing Boredom and Conflict during a Playdate, Part 1
5 Ending Business

Handling Oppositional and Argumentative
Behaviors in Children with ADHD

Handout 4.1

Using antecedents to prevent oppositional and argumentative behaviors

1 **Add positivity to your relationship with your child**
   - ❏ Increase Special Time
   - ❏ Praise often, even for small examples of positive behavior

2 **Structure commands to encourage compliance**
   - ❏ Make instructions short, as if you are speaking to a child two years younger than yours
   - ❏ Make sure your child knows, after your command, exactly what behavior they should be doing; "act nice" is too vague
   - ❏ Consider writing instructions down if it helps your child remember
   - ❏ When possible, help your child understand in a manner appropriate for their age the rationale behind why you are giving that command

3 **Structure interactions to encourage compliance**
   - ❏ Try to make sure your child is not hungry or tired when you need compliant behavior
   - ❏ Keep activities well structured, fun, and engaging—children misbehave more when they are bored

4 **Pick your battles**
   - ❏ Decide in advance what are the core rules of your house that must be followed, and discuss them with your child
   - ❏ Consider sharing with your child the reasons why you have picked these core house rules, in a manner appropriate for your child's age
   - ❏ Be consistent: Whatever the core rules are, enforce them the same way every time to prevent your child from being confused
   - ❏ Consider if you can lighten up on other rules that are less important

5 **Use humor**
   - ❏ If the defiance is mild, turn it into a joke instead
   - ❏ If the defiance is mild, try active listening to show your child you understand their side
   - ❏ Remarkably, after doing these things, your child may comply with your request

6 **Introduce a behavior plan**
   - ❏ In a situation when your child consistently misbehaves, a behavior contract may help.
   - ❏ Start with just one situation and with an easy behavior goal that your child already reaches 75% of the time

☐ Give your child a reward for making the behavior goal. Ideally reward your child with something small daily (like TV or computer time, a bedtime story) and let your child work over time to earn bigger rewards (like a new toy). Some young children find enough rewards in parental praise.

☐ After your child buys into the program, increase the difficulty of goals.

Using consequences to stop oppositional and argumentative behaviors

1 Stay calm

☐ If you keep your temper, then it makes your child's behavior less likely to escalate.

☐ It's ok for you to take a break and calm down before talking to your child if you need to.

☐ Don't argue back and forth with your child if it's not productive.

2 Stay firm

☐ If your child is breaking a core house rule, or is not meeting the behavior goal on the contract, give the consequence you said you would give.

☐ It is human nature for your child to try to test the limits and see how firm you are. Your child is not being a bad kid for doing that. Most children beg, plead, argue, make you feel guilty, say they hate you, and complain it's unfair. However, you don't want your child to learn that they can argue their way out of things.

☐ If possible, give older children (ages 9–11) some autonomy to explain their side, but ultimately you are the authority and when you are sure you have your child's best interests in mind, don't waver.

3 Follow through with the behavior plan

☐ Give the rewards in the behavior plan for meeting the behavior goals.

☐ Similarly, be firm and consistent about failing to give the rewards if the child does not meet the stated behavior goal.

4 Give positive attention when oppositional behavior stops

☐ When your child does (eventually) comply, don't back down on the consequence if you gave one for the original misbehavior, but still thank and praise your child for turning the behavior around.

☐ Don't hold grudges; follow through on whatever consequence you gave, but don't dwell on it. If you took away TV for the evening because of bad behavior, don't keep saying "bet you're bored now, huh? You should have thought of that before you acted so badly." Don't let your child watch TV, but don't rub it in.

Preventing Boredom and Conflict on Playdates

Handout 4.2

Nothing to do: The child and the peer should be discussing in advance a list of activities they both find fun and they both want to do during the playdate. Parents can help encourage their child to have this conversation.

Activity didn't work out: Parents should make sure the list of activities is okay with parents and that all materials are there. For example, the kids may decide in advance they want to go fishing, but it's not okay with the parent for them to do that. Or the kids may decide in advance they want to ride bikes, but no arrangement has been made for the peer to bring over a bike.

Game got boring: Make sure there is more than one activity to do. Talk to your child in advance about how they can tell if the peer is getting bored, and what to do about it. Also talk to your child about what they can do if they are getting bored see "Being a Good Host" (Handout 5.2).

Ran out of things to do: A first playdate might be no more than 60–90 minutes for a younger child (6–8) and 90–120 minutes for an older child (9–11). If the children like each other, they will be having fun when the time is up, and they will want to get together again.

Got tired or grumpy: Make sure your child is well-rested and not hungry before the playdate. If your child takes medication that helps with their behavior, give your child the medication. During the playdate, have a snack on hand to prepare in case you see the children getting tired or grumpy.

Siblings in the way: If possible, playdates should ideally be one-on-one between the child and peer to maximally deepen the friendship. You can make the child's room strictly off limits to the sib during a playdate, schedule a different playdate for the sib at the same time, let the sib have a treat like watching a favorite video, or have another adult attend to the sib.

Off-limits toys: Before the peer comes over, put away anything that your child does not want the guest to play with, such as special toys, breakable models, etc. A good place to put these things is in the parent's bedroom. If you have a rule against video games during the playdate, put away all the games in advance.

Couldn't agree: Before the peer comes over, go over the rules about "Being a Good Host" with your child.

PARENTAL
FRIENDSHIP
COACHING

Talking to a Peer about What to Do on a Playdate

Handout 4.3

1 **Identify a few potential activities with your child to do on the playdate.** These should be activities that are feasible to arrange, not too expensive, that your child thinks are fun and that you are okay with your child and the peer doing.

2 **Determine where your child and the peer can have this conversation.** Options are at school or wherever your child and the peer see each other, in the neighborhood, or over the phone (texting, calling).

3 **Teach your child to invite the peer for a playdate.** Your child can say, "I wanted to know if you would like to come over and play sometime."

4 **Teach your child how to do "Play Detective."** In this activity, your child will find out about what the peer likes so they can figure out what might be fun for them to play together. Children can say, "I want to find out what kinds of things you like to play," "what do you want to do when you come over?" "so what things do you like?" or "do you like biking?" if biking was one of the activities that you and your child came up with.

5 **Set rules of behavior for the conversation.** Here's a chance to work on conversational skills. Make sure your child isn't silly. If your child has a problem with talking too much, then make a rule about that. If your child has a problem with talking too little, then brainstorm some questions first with your child and make a rule that your child has to ask five questions.

6 **Do a practice conversation** (if you think your child needs this). A cousin who is a similar age is good, or a sibling. Your child should practice "Play Detective" with them.

7 **Have the real conversation.** Have your child talk to the peer. After the child and the peer come up with things they would like to do together, then you should arrange the details with the other parent.

8 **Praise your child for trying no matter what the outcome.** Make sure to find lots of things to praise, and give any corrective feedback if relevant. If you were able to observe the conversation, let your child know how well they followed the rules of behavior and how they did as a "Play Detective."

PARENTAL
FRIENDSHIP
COACHING

Session 4 Homework List

Homework 4.1	Handling Oppositional Behavior Practice
	Experiment with trying out one of the things on the list to handle oppositional behavior. You should choose one new strategy that you think might work with your child. Parents should individualize this homework assignment to pick the strategy they want to work on.
	The suggestion that I plan to try is: _____
Date	Observations (child reactions, successes, obstacles, etc.)
Homework 4.2	Practice Talking with a Peer about What to Do on a Playdate
	If your child has never done this before or if you suspect this will not go well the first time around, they can have a practice conversation. Talking to a cousin about the same age as your child or a sibling may be a good idea for practice. Once your child has the hang of it, the goal is for your child to try having this conversation with a peer who you have identified as a potential friend, and asking them for a playdate.
Date	Observations (child reactions, successes, obstacles, etc.)
Homework 4.3	Continue Relationship-Building
	Continue Special Time, active listening, praise, etc. The idea is that these strategies will fade more into the background as they become second-nature.
Date	Observations (child reactions, successes, obstacles, etc.)

Playdate Progress:

For this week, work on hosting a playdate for your child. The skills we have learned so far are as follows:

- With your child, discuss who you would like to invite for a playdate.
- (New Skill) Help your child talk to the friend to decide what to play.
- (New Skill) Prepare fun activities for the playdate.
- (New Skill) Ensure your child is not tired or hungry before the playdate.

PARENTAL
FRIENDSHIP
COACHING

Session 4 Parent Satisfaction Form

Did you complete your homework assignments over the previous week?

Homework 3.1: Continue effective praise and feedback.
Yes   No

Homework 3.2: Have a discussion with your child about a peer to invite
over for a playdate
Yes   No

Homework 3.3: Continue Special Time, active listening, etc.
Yes   No

Playdate Progress: Since the last session until today
    How many playdates did you host for your child? _____
      In this playdate(s), I worked on (check all that apply)
      ___Discussing with my child who to invite for a playdate
    How many playdates did your child attend as a guest?_____

Since the last session until today, approximately how much time (if any)
did you spend *outside of session* doing homework assignments, thinking
about what was discussed, looking over the handouts, or discussing topics
from the session with other people?

_____ minutes in total

How useful did you find the session this week (circle one)?

1----------2----------3----------4----------5----------6----------7
Not at all   Medium   Very much

Comments, questions, or suggestions:

Name: _____

*Thank you for your honest feedback; it helps me better serve your needs and
helps to improve the program for future parents.*

Session 5 Topics

1 **Review of Homework**
2 **Video Recording Review (Optional)**
3 **Helping Your Child Learn Good Friendship Skills, Part 1**
4 **Preventing Boredom and Conflict during a Playdate, Part 2**
5 **Ending Business**

Helping Your Child Improve Game-Playing Skills

Handout 5.1

Qualities of interactive games or toys

Good interactive games or toys are fun to play only (or mainly) if they are played with someone else. Your child should have at least one inside and one outside interactive game or toy with these qualities:

- Requires at least two persons to play so that your child will be encouraged to interact with a peer
- Does not encourage aggression (e.g., water pistols) unless your child will behave in a controlled way with this toy
- Is fun for you and your child to play, because you will be teaching it to your child so you might as well enjoy it
- Has simple rules so that your child won't need much help to play with a friend and won't lose patience learning the game
- Does not take too long to play, so it ends before your child tends to lose interest in activities; the younger the child, the shorter the game should be
- Is inexpensive so that it won't be a great loss if it isn't played or it breaks

If your child doesn't know enough interactive games

Play the game and teach your child the rules. Keep your tone upbeat and fun. Try to have a good time with your child. If your child has difficulties with attention, don't expect that they will remember all the rules right away.

- It's ok to let your child win at first. It will encourage your child to like the game in the beginning, and it will keep competition out of the relationship between the two of you.
- Once your child gets better at the game and is playing it more seriously, then start challenging them so that sometimes you win and sometimes they win.
- Kids will sometimes say when they start getting good, "Are you letting me win? Let's play for real." If your child says this, then it is definitely time to start challenging them.
- Even if your child does not ask, once they learn the game well enough you should start challenging them, because that is what a peer will do.

If your child has behavior problems during games

If your child likes to cheat, makes up their own rules, does not notice when peers are bored or angry, or does other behaviors in games that are off-putting to peers, address these behaviors when you see them. Remind your child in a nonangry tone of voice:

- Parent: It's no fun to play unless you stick by the rules.
- Parent: It's no fun to play if I don't get to move where I want to.

- Parent: I'm not having fun anymore, and it would be really nice of you to ask me if I want to play something else.

It might help to discuss the behavior problem with your child in advance of playing so that the child knows what to work on:

PARENT: I know that it can upset you when you are losing, so when we play I want to see you try your best to be a good sport.
CHILD: Ok.
PARENT: What could you do to show you are a good sport?
CHILD: Be nice.
PARENT: That's right, even if you are losing you would keep playing. What could you say?
CHILD: Say "good game."
PARENT: Good idea! Say "good game" no matter who wins.

PARENT: How do you think you could tell if your friend is getting bored of the game?
CHILD: I don't know, maybe he'd be looking across the room.
PARENT: Great! Any other ideas?
CHILD: Maybe he'd seem like he wasn't excited anymore.
PARENT: I think that's exactly right. If you saw this happening, what could you do?
CHILD: Ask him if he wants to play something else.
PARENT: That sounds great. Why don't we practice this at our next family game night. At some point I am going to act bored and I want to see if you can pick up on that and if you'll ask me if I want to play something else, okay?

Remember to praise when your child shows any improvement in these behaviors:

- Parent: I really appreciate that you let me take my turn.
- Parent: That's being a good sport when you said "nice job" to me after my turn.
- Parent: It was considerate of you to ask me if I wanted to play something else.
- Parent: You were patient when I was taking a long time to decide. That's being a good friend.

Even if your child doesn't improve the behaviors the first time, don't get angry or discouraged, just keep trying. Learning any new skill takes time and repetition. Be patient with your child and with yourself.

Being a Good Host

Handout 5.2

1 **The guest is always right**
   A good host tries hard to make the guest feel welcome. Whenever there is a question, the host should let the guest go first and have their way. If the guest is bored and wants to play something else, the host should try to go along with it.

2 **If the host doesn't like the activity, suggest doing something else in a polite way**
   Impolite way: This is boring
   Better: Can we play something else?
   Best: Can we play Sorry next after we each get one more out?
   Impolite way: I'm not being the mom anymore.
   Better: Can you please be the mom for a little while?
   Best: Can we play it this way until the end of this story, and then we'll switch so you be the mom, okay?

3 **Don't criticize the guest**
   Impolite way: You're cheating
   Better: Can we make a rule that…
   Impolite: That's a boring idea
   Better: How about we play (name something else)?
   Impolite way: You messed up right there
   Better: Good try (or say nothing)

4 **Be loyal to the guest**
   Don't invite another child in to play while the guest is still there. Don't leave the guest alone for a long period of time. Check to see if the guest is having fun and try to make sure the guest is having a good time.

5 **Say a nice goodbye to the guest**
   When it is time for the guest to leave, tell the guest thank you for coming. If you had a fun time with them, it is nice to let the guest know that.

Session 5 Homework List

Homework 5.1	Game Skills Practice
	If your child doesn't know or like enough games, pick a new game and play it with your child. If your child has game knowledge but you are concerned about their behavior when playing, pick a game your child already knows and play it with them. Generate the situations where your child shows problems and talk to your child about how to handle them. Use effective praise and corrective feedback to teach your child how to respond appropriately. The activity I plan to try is: _____
Date	Observations (child reactions, successes, obstacles, etc.)
Homework 5.2	Continue Relationship-Building
	Continue Special Time, active listening, praise/corrective feedback, etc.
Date	Observations (child reactions, successes, obstacles, etc.)

Playdate Progress:
For this week, work on hosting a playdate for your child. The skills we have learned so far are as follows:

- With your child, discuss who you would like to invite for a playdate.
- Help your child talk to the friend to decide what to play.
- Prepare fun activities for the playdate.
- Ensure your child is not tired or hungry before the playdate.
- (New Skill) Before the playdate, talk to your child about being a good host.
- (New Skill) Put away any toys that are likely to cause conflict.

Session 5 Parent Satisfaction Form

Did you complete your homework assignments over the previous week?

Homework 4.1: Try a suggestion to handle oppositional and argumentative behaviors
Yes   No

Homework 4.2: Help your child talk with a peer about what to do on a playdate
Yes   No

Homework 4.3: Continue Special Time, active listening, praise, etc.
Yes   No

Playdate Progress: Since the last session until today
    How many playdates did you host for your child? _____
        In this playdate(s), I worked on (check all that apply)
    ___Discussing with my child who to invite for a playdate
    ___Helping my child talk to the friend to decide what to play
    ___Preparing fun activities for the playdate
        ___Helping ensure my child is not tired or hungry before the playdate
    How many playdates did your child attend as a guest? _____

Since the last session until today, approximately how much time (if any) did you spend *outside of session* doing homework assignments, thinking about what was discussed, looking over the handouts, or discussing topics from the session with other people?

_____ minutes in total

How useful did you find the session this week (circle one)?

    1----------2----------3----------4----------5----------6----------7
    Not at all   Medium   Very much

Comments, questions, or suggestions:

Name: _____

Thank you for your honest feedback; it helps me better serve your needs and helps to improve the program for future parents.

Session 6 Topics

1 **Review of Homework**
2 **Helping Your Child Learn Good Friendship Skills, Part 2**
3 **Handling Boredom and Conflict during the Playdate when Best Efforts Fail**
4 **Video Recording Review (Optional)**
5 **Ending Business**

PARENTAL
FRIENDSHIP
COACHING

Common Mistakes in Conversational Skills
Made by Children with ADHD

Handout 6.1

1 Talking too much
- ☐ Talking most of the conversation without asking the peer any questions
- ☐ Talking too long about things the peer is not interested in
- ☐ Not realizing when the peer wants to talk about something else
- ☐ Interrupting when the peer is trying to talk
- ☐ Bragging about themselves, their abilities, or their possessions
- ☐ Saying rude, critical, or insensitive things to the peer (can be unintentionally or without realizing it)
- ☐ Changing the subject often from one thing to another
- ☐ Insisting that everyone has to talk about what they want to
- ☐ Having trouble sitting down and talking (relative to what other children their same age and gender do), instead preferring to run around

2 Talking too little
- ☐ Tending to be reticent and slow to respond
- ☐ Missing social cues
- ☐ Unable to keep up with the quick back-and-forth pace of conversation
- ☐ Daydreaming, off in their own world, so they do not know what is going on in the conversation
- ☐ Appearing sluggish, apathetic, and not enthusiastic
- ☐ Failing to show interest in what the peer is interested in
- ☐ Not seeming excited to be around the peer
- ☐ Appearing disengaged
- ☐ Genuinely not knowing what to say; they just don't have the words or the social skills
- ☐ Losing interest in the middle of the conversation
- ☐ Having no idea what they just talked about a few minutes or hours later—as if the conversation never even happened

3 Talking about inappropriate things or at inappropriate times
- ☐ Sharing things that are too personal, for example, how they got kicked out of a school
- ☐ Talking about things other kids find gross and don't want to hear about
- ☐ Asking their peers questions that are too personal and that peers don't want to answer

☐ Telling lies to get attention from peers
☐ Trying repeatedly to talk to peers who dislike them, which annoys peers further
☐ Saying things like "I love you" to peers who are only acquaintances
☐ Trying to engage in conversation with peers while the teacher or adult is talking, or at another inappropriate time where it gets them into trouble

Conversational Skills Worksheet

Handout 6.2

The conversational skill I chose to work on is:

Some ANTECEDENTS I can try are:

1

2.

3.

If the conversational skill improves at all (even if it is not perfect), I will say to my child:

If the conversational skill doesn't improve, then I will try:

What will be the hardest about this plan is:

Instructing Your Child during a Playdate

Handout 6.3

If your child is misbehaving during a playdate, you have four choices about what to do.

1 **Ignore it completely in the moment.** You may decide to talk to your child about it afterward once the guest has left. This is a better choice if:
   - ❏ The behavior problem is fairly mild
   - ❏ The peer doesn't seem to notice or mind the behavior problem
   - ❏ Your child does not typically show this behavior problem
   - ❏ Your child is easily embarrassed

2 **Try to diffuse the situation in a casual way, which may make them forget about their conflict, kind of like "changing the subject."** You could talk to your child about it afterward once the guest has left. This is a better choice if:
   - ❏ The behavior problem is fairly mild
   - ❏ The peer is not very mad
   - ❏ Your child is not very mad
   - ❏ They have gotten stuck arguing about something silly
   - ❏ Your child is easily embarrassed

Example: Child and peer have been playing cars, and they have been playing well up to now. Child starts saying that the red car can go the fastest. The peer disagrees and says the black car can. Neither will let it go. They are starting to get worked up about this disagreement. The parent interrupts and says to both kids "Want to come in the kitchen and let's have a snack?" Both kids come happily and later go back to playing well because they have forgotten about their argument.

3 **Say something quickly to your child during the playdate.** This is a better choice if:
   - ❏ The misbehavior is mild to moderate
   - ❏ The peer has noticed and is bothered by the misbehavior
   - ❏ Overall the playdate seems to be going well up until now
   - ❏ Your child and the peer are younger (age 6–8)
   - ❏ Your child is not very easily embarrassed
   - ❏ You can give your suggestion in one sentence or less
   - ❏ Your child is unlikely to argue with you about the suggestion

Example: Child and peer (age 6) are playing and peer reaches to touch the doll the child is holding. Child pulls the doll away. Overall, the two children seem to be getting along and like each other. The parent bends down and whispers in the child's ear, "Remember to take turns and share your doll."

Then, the parent backs up to see if the child obeys. If the child doesn't obey, the parent can always try a different plan.

4 **Pull your child aside into another room and talk to them.** This is a better choice if:
   ☐ The misbehavior is moderate to severe
   ☐ There's been more than one incident of conflict or tense moments in this playdate already
   ☐ The peer has noticed your child's misbehavior already
   ☐ The peer seems bothered by the misbehavior
   ☐ This is a repeated problem that your child shows with peers (and therefore less likely to change with a subtle strategy)
   ☐ Your child and the peer are older (age 9–11)
   ☐ You need more than one sentence to explain to your child why the behavior is a problem
   ☐ You suspect your child may argue with you about your instruction

Example: Child and peer (age 9) are playing Sorry and the child tells the peer that the peer made a stupid move. The child is now laughing and the peer looks mad.

PARENT: (from doorway) I need to talk to you for a minute. Please come here. (Child comes). Thank you.
PARENT: (to peer) We will be right back.
CHILD: Awww, he just doesn't know how to play.
PARENT: Remember the rules of a good host?
CHILD: (silence)
PARENT: Don't criticize who?
CHILD: The guest.
PARENT: That's right. Now what can you say to your guest instead?
CHILD: (grumpily) Say nothing.
PARENT: That's a great idea! Saying nothing when your guest makes a bad move would be the polite thing to do. I want you to try that out, please.
CHILD: I guess so.
PARENT: Thanks so much, I really like how you are trying hard to be a good host. Now you can go back and play.

To call the child out of the room in a subtle way, the parent could also have said "I need your help with something quickly, please."

For recurring behavior problems, parents and children can also set up a "secret signal" in advance by which parents can remind children that they need to change the behavior that they had discussed but the peer does not know that this reminder is occurring.

Rules to remember when instructing your child during a playdate:

DO: Praise when your child agrees to change their behavior, even if your child sounds grumpy and half-hearted about it

DO: Speak in a low volume and nonangry tone of voice

DO: Make the feedback as private as the situation will allow

DO: Be encouraging and sound like you believe your child can turn around the behavior (if you honestly don't believe your child is capable of it, then have a shorter playdate, a different activity, or a different peer over)

DO: Discuss with your child after the guest leaves what they did well and thank your child for their efforts; remember to praise

DO: Keep the discussion as short as possible; get straight to the point about the behavior that needs to be changed and try to get your child back in with the peer as soon as you can

DO: End the discussion with a clear plan of action so that your child knows exactly what behavior to do instead

DO: Think about how you might try harder to use antecedents to prevent this behavior next time

DON'T: Criticize your child's character

DON'T: Talk about times in the past that your child has also broken these rules

DON'T: Yell or lose your temper, or show frustration

DON'T: Send away the guest or threaten to do this for your child's misbehavior, unless the child and guest are doing something physically dangerous. Find another way to take something away from your child (e.g., no TV that evening) that doesn't involve the guest.

DON'T: Ask your child a question when you want your child to obey the rule (e.g., don't you think it would be better for you to share the doll, okay?)

Session 6 Homework List

Homework 6.1	**Practice Conversational Skills**
	Try out one of the suggestions to practice conversational skills that you wrote on the worksheet.
	The activity I plan to try is: _____
Date	**Observations** (child reactions, successes, obstacles, etc.)
Homework 6.2	**Continue Relationship-Building**
	Continue Special Time, active listening, praise/corrective feedback, etc.
Date	**Observations** (child reactions, successes, obstacles, etc.)

Playdate Progress:

For this week, work on hosting a playdate for your child. The skills we have learned so far are as follows:

- With your child, discuss who you would like to invite for a playdate.
- Help your child talk to the friend to decide what to play.
- Prepare fun activities for the playdate.
- Ensure your child is not tired or hungry before the playdate.
- Before the playdate, talk to your child about being a good host.
- Put away any toys that are likely to cause conflict.
- (New Skill) Intervene in the playdate to stop early signs of boredom.
- (New Skill) Intervene in the playdate to stop early signs of conflict.

Session 6 Parent Satisfaction Form

Did you complete your homework assignments over the previous week?

Homework 5.1: Do an activity to improve game-playing skills
Yes No

Homework 5.2: Continue Special Time, active listening, praise, etc.
Yes No

Playdate Progress: Since the last session until today
    How many playdates did you host for your child? _____
        In this playdate(s), I worked on (check all that apply)
        ___Discussing with my child who to invite for a playdate
        ___Helping my child talk to the friend to decide what to play
        ___Preparing fun activities for the playdate
        ___Ensuring my child is not tired or hungry before the playdate
        ___Talking to my child in advance about being a good host
        ___Putting away any toys likely to cause conflict
    How many playdates did your child attend as a guest? _____

Since the last session until today, approximately how much time (if any) did you spend *outside of session* doing homework assignments, thinking about what was discussed, looking over the handouts, or discussing topics from the session with other people?

_____ minutes in total

How useful did you find the session this week (circle one)?

    1----------2----------3----------4----------5----------6----------7
    Not at all   Medium   Very much

Comments, questions, or suggestions:

Name: _____

Thank you for your honest feedback; it helps me better serve your needs and helps to improve the program for future parents.

Session 7 Topics

1 **Review of Homework**
2 **Helping Your Child Learn Good Friendship Skills, Part 3**
3 **Giving Effective Feedback after the Playdate**
4 **Video Recording Review (Optional)**
5 **Ending Business**

Dealing with Negative Emotions

Handout 7.1

1 Helping your child to recognize when negative emotions are arising
Negative emotions are natural for kids and adults. But the goal is for children to notice when they begin to feel negative emotions so that they are not surprised by them all of a sudden, and so they can work on handling them before the emotions take over.

- Ask your child how they can tell when they are starting to feel angry or sad. Look out for body signs like heart racing, fists clenched, stomach in knots, face hot, sad, or mad thoughts.
- While watching TV or a movie, or reading a book, ask your child how the characters are feeling and how your child knew that the character was feeling this.
- You might share your own experiences about when you are starting to feel angry or sad and how you can tell.
- Some children like the labels of "green light" for no negative emotion, "yellow light" for starting to feel the emotion, and "red light" for a strong negative emotion that stops everything. The idea is to use "yellow light" as a warning.

2 Helping your child to come up with plans for self-regulation
Sometimes just noticing the negative emotion in Step 1 is enough to help kids feel better. However, it can also help kids to have strategies they can use to calm down when they start to feel negative emotions. Discuss these strategies with your child at a time when they are not upset.

- Calm countdown: Counting backward from 10. Children can do this out loud at home to let parents know they are working on calming down and silently at school.
- Thinking cool thoughts: Cool thoughts are meant to help cool down the situation.
- For younger kids:
"I won't get upset"
"I can stay cool"
"It's just a game"
- For older kids:
"I won't sink to their level"
"I am in control of my emotions"
"I can be the bigger person"
- Taking a break: Sometimes it helps to go to the bathroom or step away from the situation to clear your head. This can be done with the calm countdown.
- Deep breaths: This is something parents and kids can practice together. Put your hands over your tummy and practice breathing in and out slowly, and feeling your belly inflate and deflate like a balloon.

Debriefing after a Playdate

Handout 7.2

After the guest has left, give your child some feedback about their behavior. This is a good opportunity for your child to learn which behaviors to continue and which behaviors to change so that your child can do a better job making friends on the next playdate.

Here are some points to remember in your conversation with your child:

- Your child may be defensive initially, expecting that you will say negative things.
- Remember to praise your child about specific behaviors that were good.
- Aim for a 4:1 ratio of praise to corrections; to do this you may have to praise for 30% correct or ignore lower priority problem behaviors.
- If your child got into an argument with the peer, start by using active listening about your child's feelings. If possible, empathize with your child about ways in which the peer could have done a better job too. This way it doesn't come off as you are one-sidedly criticizing your child.
- Stay calm and keep your temper. If you feel yourself getting upset, it's okay to take a break and debrief with your child later.
- With corrective feedback, stick to the problem behavior your saw this time and try not to bring up things in the past.
- Ask your child for suggestions about what to do better next time (especially with older children). If your child has trouble coming up with suggestions, you can give your child two better ways to handle the situation and ask which one they would like to do.
- Keep an optimistic and encouraging tone; communicate that you think your child can achieve what you are asking.
- It's okay to have some quiet moments.
- Be patient with yourself and with your child's progress; learning to make friends takes practice, just like learning any new skill.

Session 7 Homework List

Homework 7.1	Practice Dealing with Negative Emotions
	Have this discussion or practice with your child about dealing with negative emotions.
	The activity I plan to try is: _____
Date	Observations (child reactions, successes, obstacles, etc.)
Homework 7.2	Continue Relationship-Building
	Continue Special Time, active listening, praise/corrective feedback, etc.
Date	Observations (child reactions, successes, obstacles, etc.)

Playdate Progress:

For this week, work on hosting a playdate for your child. The skills we have learned so far are as follows:

- With your child, discuss who you would like to invite for a playdate.
- Help your child talk to the friend to decide what to play.
- Prepare fun activities for the playdate.
- Ensure your child is not tired or hungry before the playdate.
- Before the playdate, talk to your child about being a good host.
- Put away any toys that are likely to cause conflict.
- Intervene in the playdate to stop early signs of boredom.
- Intervene in the playdate to stop early signs of conflict.
- (New Skill) Debrief with your child after the playdate.

Session 7 Parent Satisfaction Form

Did you complete your homework assignments over the previous week?

Homework 6.1: Try one thing to help your child develop better conversation skills
Yes   No

Homework 6.2: Continue Special Time, active listening, praise, etc.
Yes   No

Playdate Progress: Since the last session until today
How many playdates did you host for your child? _____
In this playdate(s), I worked on (check all that apply)
___Discussing with my child who to invite for a playdate
___Helping my child talk to the friend to decide what to play
___Preparing fun activities for the playdate
___Ensuring my child is not tired or hungry before the playdate
___Talking to my child in advance about being a good host
___Putting away any toys likely to cause conflict
___Intervening in the playdate to stop early signs of boredom
___Intervening in the playdate to stop early signs of conflict
How many playdates did your child attend as a guest? _____

Since the last session until today, approximately how much time (if any) did you spend *outside of session* doing homework assignments, thinking about what was discussed, looking over the handouts, or discussing topics from the session with other people?

_____ minutes in total

How useful did you find the session this week (circle one)?

1----------2----------3----------4----------5----------6----------7
Not at all   Medium   Very much

Comments, questions, or suggestions:

Name: _____

Thank you for your honest feedback; it helps me better serve your needs and helps to improve the program for future parents.

Session 8 Topics

1 **Review of Homework**
2 **Preparing for a Playdate as a Guest**
3 **Picking Up Your Child from a Playdate as a Guest**
4 **Video Recording Review (Optional)**
5 **Ending Business**

Being a Good Guest

Handout 8.1

1 **Say hello to the host and the host's parents when you arrive.** It's polite to greet them and helpful to let them know you are there (if they don't already know).

2 **Follow the rules of the host's house.** Even if the rules are different from the rules at home, when you are in the host's house you need to follow their rules.

3 **Ask permission before you touch something, play with something, or eat something, unless the host offered it to you.** It's not your house and the things belong to the host.

4 **If the host's parents say something to you that you think is unfair, try to explain your side of it once. If that doesn't work, be quiet.** You can tell your parents about it later. If you think it's really unfair, you don't have to go over to the host's house again.

5 **When you are leaving, say thank you to the host and to the host's parents for having you over.** Also say something nice, like that you had fun playing.

Encouraging a Structured Playdate as a Guest

Handout 8.2

Example 1

(Parent 2 is concerned that Carly will not behave well in a long, unstructured playdate but does not want to communicate this to Parent 1 at this time).

Parent 1: We'd like to have Carly come over on Saturday.

Parent 2: Carly will be so excited, thanks so much! What did you have in mind?

Parent 1: Oh hmmm, I don't know, maybe she could come over in the morning and hang out until we have our family barbeque that afternoon. And there's a pool out there too.

Parent 2: That sounds fun. We have a bunch of stuff to do on Saturday morning; any chance that I could drop her off for the barbeque? What time would that start?

Parent 1: Sure, we'll probably fire up the grill around 2 and then cook around 3. Maybe the girls can go swimming before the cookout?

Parent 2: That sounds perfect. I'll drop Carly off with her bathing suit at 2 and then check in around 4 to see if she is all done eating. It is so kind of you to invite her and she will really have fun.

Example 2

(Parent 2 is concerned that D'Shawn will not behave well when playing competitive video games, and wants to let Parent 1 know this without seeming overly concerned or controlling).

Parent 1: Tyler says that he and D'Shawn want to play this weekend. I thought I would take them to Playland arcade.

Parent 2: Oh, D'Shawn will like that. I also know he likes Tyler and has said a lot of good things about him.

Parent 1: Great! How is Saturday afternoon?

Parent 2: That will be good. D'Shawn will be over the moon with excitement. By the way, sometimes he can get overstimulated with video games, especially when they're competitive, so if you're seeing that feel free to make them off limits for a time so he can cool down.

Parent 1: Actually, Tyler gets that way too; I'll just make them off limits for both the boys.

Parent 2: Awesome. Should I drop him off at your house or just meet at Playland?

PARENTAL
FRIENDSHIP
COACHING

Picking Up Your Child from a Playdate as a Guest

Handout 8.3

In order to encourage the probability that your child will be asked over again:

1 **Make sure your child follows the rules of a good guest**. Talk to your child about them in advance. If necessary, set up a reward plan for following the rules well.

2 **Pick up your child personally, if possible**. Try to have a face-to-face interaction where you thank the other parent for hosting your child and get to know the other parent a bit better. If picking up from the other parent's house, park the car and go to the door (instead of having your child run to the car).

3 **Check in with the host parent about your child's behavior**. If your child has displayed bad behavior, the host parent may not tell you unless you specifically ask. Instead, they will just not invite your child over again. Ask in a way that makes you seem like you are on top of your child's behavior, but not overly concerned.

4 **Respond well to the host parent's feedback about your child**. Be open-minded and stay calm and nondefensive. Show that you take the feedback seriously without appearing upset. The amount you should seem concerned should depend on how objectively problematic your child's behavior was.

Session 8 Homework List

Homework 8.1	**Continue Relationship-Building** **Continue Special Time, active listening, praise/corrective feedback, etc.**
Date	**Observations** (child reactions, successes, obstacles, etc.)

Playdate Progress:

For this week, work on hosting a playdate for your child. The skills we have learned so far are as follows:

- With your child, discuss who you would like to invite for a playdate.
- Help your child talk to the friend to decide what to play.
- Prepare fun activities for the playdate.
- Ensure your child is not tired or hungry before the playdate.
- Before the playdate, talk to your child about being a good host.
- Put away any toys that are likely to cause conflict.
- Intervene in the playdate to stop early signs of boredom.
- Intervene in the playdate to stop early signs of conflict.
- Debrief with your child after the playdate.
- (New Skill) Prepare your child to be a good guest.
- (New Skill) Check in with the parent of the peer about your child's behavior.

PARENTAL FRIENDSHIP COACHING

Session 8 Parent Satisfaction Form

Did you complete your homework assignments over the previous week?

Homework 7.1: Try an activity to help your child deal with negative emotions
Yes   No

Homework 7.2: Continue Special Time, active listening, praise, etc.
Yes   No

Playdate Progress: Since the last session until today
How many playdates did you host for your child? _____
In this playdate(s), I worked on (check all that apply)
___Discussing with my child who to invite for a playdate
___Helping my child talk to the friend to decide what to play
___Preparing fun activities for the playdate
___Ensuring my child is not tired or hungry before the playdate
___Talking to my child in advance about being a good host
___Putting away any toys likely to cause conflict
___Intervening in the playdate to stop early signs of boredom
___Intervening in the playdate to stop early signs of conflict
___Debriefing with my child after the playdate
How many playdates did your child attend as a guest? _____

Since the last session until today, approximately how much time (if any) did you spend *outside of session* doing homework assignments, thinking about what was discussed, looking over the handouts, or discussing topics from the session with other people?

_____ minutes in total

How useful did you find the session this week (circle one)?

1----------2----------3----------4----------5----------6----------7
Not at all   Medium   Very much

Comments, questions, or suggestions:

Name: _____

Thank you for your honest feedback; it helps me better serve your needs and helps to improve the program for future parents.

Session 9 Topics

1 **Review of Homework**
2 **Meeting New Friends**
3 **Parent-to-Parent Networking**
4 **Video Recording Review (Optional)**
5 **Ending Business**

How Children Join Others at Play

Handout 9.1

Follows rules of etiquette	Doesn't know rules—Doesn't join	Breaks rules
Watches other children playing first and approaches to show interest	Off by self, doesn't approach	Jumps into game, starts playing without knowing what is going on
After watching for a while, says something nice like "nice shot, good move"	Doesn't watch closely enough	Criticizes, tries to take over, "you should have moved there; now go here"
Waits for a pause in the game and then asks to join	Never asks to join, does not seem interested in the other children	Intrusively joins without checking to see if it's okay or not at a good time
Asks to join the side of the game that needs the most help, like the side with the fewest players	Never asks to join, does not seem interested in the other children	Tries to join the winning side
Asks the child who owns the game or toy to join	Never asks to join, does not seem interested in the other children	Takes the game or toy and starts controlling it
If allowed to join, follows the rules of the game	Either does not join, or can't remember the rules	Breaks the rules of the game or tries to change the rules
Accepts no for an answer if ignored or not allowed to join, and does something else without seeming upset	Never asks to join, does not seem interested in the other children	Complains, threatens to tell the teacher, whines, cries, or gets angry

Coaching Your Child to Join Others at Play

Handout 9.2

1   Select a safe place where many children play
- ☐ A local playground or a schoolyard where children organize their own games is good.
- ☐ Or, sign your child up for an organized activity (such as a sports team or art class) where your child will interact with new peers.
- ☐ You can also pick an existing organized activity that your child is part of, but doesn't talk to everyone in the activity on a regular basis or has not been skillful in integrating with the peers in that activity.
- ☐ Pick a place where you are comfortable with the children who play there.
- ☐ If you don't already have a place in mind, scout one out before your take your child on Step 2.

2   Watch a group of children at the playground or in the organized activity
- ☐ If you are encouraging your child to approach a group of children that they don't usually interact with, pick children who are about as skilled as your child in the game/activity they are playing, are the same age or slightly younger than your child, and are the same gender, unless it is a mixed gender group already.
- ☐ On a playground, stand about 20 feet away from the group with your child. Check in with your child to make sure your child understands what the kids are playing and the rules of the game.
- ☐ In an organized activity, you might stand at the entrance with your child to do this check in.

3   Help your child think of how to join in
- ☐ Tell (or review) the etiquette rules with your child.
- ☐ Make sure your child has a plan for when to join in, and what to say.
- ☐ Review with your child what to do if turned down.
- ☐ Encourage your child to be a good sport in playing the game, to use good conversational skills, or to do a good job handling negative emotions. If you have already been practicing these friendship skills, your child will have a good model of how to do this.

4   Encourage your child to try to join in
- ☐ Don't stand next to your child when your child goes up to the peers. It will look strange to the peers.
- ☐ You might sit on a bench a few feet away and pull out a magazine and pretend to read, in a playground situation.
- ☐ In an organized activity, you might stand with the rest of the parents (if there is a parent section), or stand in the back of the room, or on the side of the field.

❑ You want to be close enough so you are able to watch what happens when your child tries to join, but you don't want to look like you are watching what happens.

5   If your child was successful at joining, end the participation on a good note

❑ If your child tends to argue with peers, then you might want to pull your child out of the interaction before that happens. Your child can always play with them again.

❑ If things are going well, then let your child play until the game ends.

❑ Praise your child for the specific behaviors they did well.

❑ You might go over some potential things they could do next time; be sure to use the principles of effective corrective feedback.

❑ Praise your child for trying to join and to meet new peers, this takes courage.

6   If your child wasn't successful at joining, support and encourage your child

❑ First use active listening if your child is disappointed by this.

❑ Remind your child to not take it personally.

❑ Praise your child for the specific behaviors they did well.

❑ You might go over some potential things they could do next time; be sure to use the principles of effective corrective feedback.

❑ Praise your child for trying to join and to meet new peers, this takes courage.

7   As time goes on, arrange playdates for your child with potential friends

❑ Once your child has had a chance to get to know the other peers, ask your child if they would like to have a playdate with anyone.

❑ Determine if you agree that the peer identified by your child is a good potential friend.

❑ Introduce yourself to the parents of the peer.

❑ If you are comfortable with the peer and the parents of the peer, have your child invite that peer for a playdate.

PARENTAL
FRIENDSHIP
COACHING

Networking with Other Parents

Handout 9.3

Possible ways to meet other parents

1   Volunteer to help out in your child's classroom.
2   Volunteer to help out in your child's extracurricular activity such as sports, scouting.
3   Stop by and observe during the extracurricular activity, game, etc. and stand where the other parents are standing.
4   If you pick your child up at school or an organized activity, chat with other parents while you are waiting.
5   Join the parent–teacher organization or parent committee at your child's school.
6   Consider joining parent groups on social media for parents in your neighborhood/local area.
7   Throw a party for everyone in your child's class, extracurricular activity, etc.
8   Throw a block party for neighborhood families. Have appetizers and lemonade; have popsicles in the summer or smores in the winter for an inexpensive treat. A BBQ is a more expensive option, but you could also ask families to bring their own things to grill while you provide the grill and condiments.
9   When your child has a playdate, chat up the other parent during the pick up or drop off.
10   Bring cookies, lemonade, or snacks to an event (if permitted) for other parents and kids there; if you came to observe your child's sports game, you could bring cookies and share them.
11   Take pictures of your child and teammates at a sports event or activity. Give pictures of the team to other parents, or give other parents good pictures of their children. If you use a digital camera and email the pictures, this won't cost any money.

Possible conversation openers with other parents

1   Say "Hi, I'm Robert, Amanda's dad." Typically, the other parent will respond with their name and tell you who their child is.
2   Work in a compliment about the other parent's child, if it's fitting and genuine.
3   Make small-talk about the game or the event. For instance, if they have a championship game coming up, you can talk about how excited your child is for that or how you hope the weather will be good. Keep the mood and the tone light.
4   At this first meeting, try not to talk about problems your child or your family is having.

5 Don't feel pressure to make a deep or strong contact out of this first meeting. If you happen to hit it off with the other parent, great, but don't go into the interaction with that expectation. The next time you see this same parent, it will be easier and you will have more to talk about.

Session 9 Homework List

Homework 9.1	Meeting New Peers
	Use one of these strategies to help your child meet new friends/broaden their social circle.
	The activity I plan to try is: _____
Date	Observations (child reactions, successes, obstacles, etc.)
Homework 9.2	Continue Relationship-Building
	Continue Special Time, active listening, praise/corrective feedback, etc.
Date	Observations (child reactions, successes, obstacles, etc.)

Playdate Progress:

For this week, work on hosting a playdate for your child. The skills we have learned so far are as follows:

- With your child, discuss who you would like to invite for a playdate.
- Help your child talk to the friend to decide what to play.
- Prepare fun activities for the playdate.
- Ensure your child is not tired or hungry before the playdate.
- Before the playdate, talk to your child about being a good host.
- Put away any toys that are likely to cause conflict.
- Intervene in the playdate to stop early signs of boredom.
- Intervene in the playdate to stop early signs of conflict.
- Debrief with your child after the playdate.
- Prepare your child to be a good guest.
- Check in with the parent of the peer about your child's behavior.

PARENTAL
FRIENDSHIP
COACHING

Session 9 Parent Satisfaction Form

Did you complete your homework assignments over the previous week?

Homework 8.1: Continue Special Time, active listening, praise, etc.
Yes   No

Playdate Progress: Since the last session until today
    How many playdates did you host for your child? _____
        In this playdate(s), I worked on (check all that apply)
        ___Discussing with my child who to invite for a playdate
        ___Helping my child talk to the friend to decide what to play
        ___Preparing fun activities for the playdate
        ___Ensuring my child is not tired or hungry before the playdate
        ___Talking to my child in advance about being a good host
        ___Putting away any toys likely to cause conflict
        ___Intervening in the playdate to stop early signs of boredom
        ___Intervening in the playdate to stop early signs of conflict
        ___Debriefing with my child after the playdate
    How many playdates did your child attend as a guest? _____
        In this playdate(s), I worked on (check all that apply)
        ___Preparing my child to be a good guest
        ___Checking in with the parent of the friend about my child's
        behavior

Since the last session until today, approximately how much time (if any) did you spend *outside of session* doing homework assignments, thinking about what was discussed, looking over the handouts, or discussing topics from the session with other people?

_____ minutes in total

How useful did you find the session this week (circle one)?

        1----------2----------3----------4----------5----------6----------7
    Not at all   Medium   Very much

Comments, questions, or suggestions:

Name: _____

Thank you for your honest feedback; it helps me better serve your needs and helps to improve the program for future parents.

Session 10 Topics

1 **Review of Homework**
2 **Deciding Whether to Have another Playdate**
3 **How to Understand another Family's Response to Your Playdate Invitation**
4 **Parting Gift**
5 **Ending Business**

Session 10 Parent Satisfaction Form

Did you complete your homework assignments over the previous week?

Homework 9.1: Try an activity to broaden your child's social circle
Yes   No

Homework 9.2: Continue Special Time, active listening, praise, etc.
Yes   No

Playdate Progress: Since the last session until today
　How many playdates did you host for your child? _____
　　In this playdate(s), I worked on (check all that apply)
　　___Discussing with my child who to invite for a playdate
　　___Helping my child talk to the friend to decide what to play
　　___Preparing fun activities for the playdate
　　___Ensuring my child is not tired or hungry before the playdate
　　___Talking to my child in advance about being a good host
　　___Putting away any toys likely to cause conflict
　　___Intervening in the playdate to stop early signs of boredom
　　___Intervening in the playdate to stop early signs of conflict
　　___Debriefing with my child after the playdate
　How many playdates did your child attend as a guest? _____
　　In this playdate(s), I worked on (check all that apply)
　　___Preparing my child to be a good guest
　　___Checking in with the parent of the friend about my child's
　　　behavior

Since the last session until today, approximately how much time (if any) did you spend *outside of session* doing homework assignments, thinking about what was discussed, looking over the handouts, or discussing topics from the session with other people?

_____ minutes in total

How useful did you find the session this week (circle one)?

　　　1----------2----------3----------4----------5----------6----------7
　　Not at all　　　　　　　　Medium　　　　　　　　Very much

Comments, questions, or suggestions:

Name: _____

Thank you for your honest feedback; it helps me better serve your needs and helps to improve the program for future parents.

Index

For Product Safety Concerns and Information please contact our EU
representative GPSR@taylorandfrancis.com
Taylor & Francis Verlag GmbH, Kaufingerstraße 24, 80331 München, Germany

www.ingramcontent.com/pod-product-compliance
Lightning Source LLC
Chambersburg PA
CBHW070334270326
41926CB00017B/3868

9 781032 118284